CAMPFIRE STORIES

THE REDWOOD COAST

CAMPFIRE STORIES

THE REDWOOD COAST

TALES & TRAVEL COMPANION

edited by

ILYSSA KYU & DAVE KYU

MOUNTAINEERS BOOKS

For our little barnacle and seal, Lula and Isla.
We'll always be your rock.

MOUNTAINEERS BOOKS is dedicated to the exploration, preservation, and enjoyment of outdoor and wilderness areas.

1001 SW Klickitat Way, Suite 201, Seattle, WA 98134
800-553-4453, www.mountaineersbooks.org

Printed in China

28 27 26 25 1 2 3 4 5

Design and layout: Melissa McFeeters

Library of Congress Cataloging-in-Publication data is on file for this title at https://lccn.loc.gov/2024947842

Printed on FSC®-certified materials

ISBN (paperback): 978-1-68051-754-5
ISBN (ebook): 978-1-68051-755-2

FSC www.fsc.org MIX Paper | Supporting responsible forestry FSC® C188448

An independent nonprofit publisher since 1960

Contents

REDWOOD COAST STORIES

EXPLORE THE REDWOOD COAST

INTRODUCTION

Behind the Redwood Curtain

STEP INSIDE ONE of Northern California's many redwood groves and you're sure to be stunned into silence. It's like stepping into an ancient library where people speak only in hushed tones as they peruse nature's catalog. Look around and below, where you'll find a carpet of crumbling fallen redwoods dotted with sword ferns, moss, fungi, sorrel, rhododendron, and huckleberry. Look up, and take in giant trees soaring toward the sky, out of view into the fog.

At the start of our trip, we found ourselves in sunny Muir Woods, the "Wilderness Next Door" to San Francisco, where we were lucky enough to talk with legendary park ranger Mia Monroe on the very last day of her fifty-year career. From there, we explored the dozens of beaches, redwood forests, trails, and state and national parks of Humboldt County, ending up 350 miles from where we had started in Jedediah Smith Redwoods State Park.

We spent a week on the North Coast, getting dumped on by buckets of winter rain, beginning each day with the ritual of applying fresh band-aids on our waterlogged heels, putting on our "dry enough" socks, and rotating between a sopping wet raincoat and an almost dry poncho... and we did it with *glee*. Each step through a redwood grove, accentuated by the sloshing of mud and water in our socks, was just as awe inspiring as we remembered from trips nearly a decade before.

This place can bring the busiest of minds into the present. One minute you've worked out the solution to world peace, and the next your focus is solely on watching fog pour through the trees or dappled sunlight chase shadows over the dancing redwood sorrel. But as we switchbacked up the Trillium Falls Trail in Redwood National Park, feeling blissfully dwarfed by massive old-growth trees, our minds wandered through the thousands of years before our visit. Passing under canopies of lichen-wrapped limbs, over logs blanketed in the vivid greens of moss and ferns, and through streams of water making their way from every direction toward the falls, we found it easy to imagine dinosaurs scratching their backs on the burls above us or lapping up water from the pools below the falls. No wonder so many films are shot in the redwoods, including the 1997 blockbuster *The Lost World: Jurassic Park*.

Though dinosaurs roamed only in our imagination, there were plenty of other terrestrial creatures in the redwoods for us to seek. Mountain lions, black bears, and coyotes all live among the trees but are seldom seen. One afternoon, though, we were lucky enough to see two of the region's male Roosevelt elk charging each other and locking antlers in a meadow outside the Prairie Creek Visitor Center.

Transfixed by the gentle drumming of rain and occasionally called to consciousness by an insistent Pacific wren, we found it difficult to hold the many truths of the Redwood Coast at the same time. Here was a place of such awe, peace, and connection to something larger than ourselves, but also a place with a human history of destruction, removal, and loss.

• ✦ •

The scale of trees here can be disorienting—measured in "Wow," "Oh, WOW!" and "Hoooooly WOW!" Redwoods grow so tall that the only people who see the tops are those who climb the trees for research. Entire worlds exist in the upper canopies of redwood trees—plants, soils, insects, worms, and birds spend their whole lives more than 200 feet above the ground. Each trunk has its own personality, with large wartlike burls at the base of mature trees (basal burls) that help anchor the trees in vulnerable soil conditions, or burls higher up that cover injuries or hold dormant buds that will sprout after a fire. We saw many living redwood trees standing mighty despite hollow caverns and crevices in their trunks, gnarly burls, and burn scars that reminded us that *these trees have seen some things*.

Redwood trees are difficult to kill—unless you chop them down. They have pest-resistant heartwood, fire-resistant bark, and the ability to regrow limbs or trunks if damaged. Even trees that have fallen produce new life. If you walk through a redwood grove, you'll notice old stumps enshrouded by a "fairy circle," a ring of trees sprouted from the roots of the parent tree.

Redwoods also live for a *very* long time—some trees in the old-growth forests of the North Coast have been there for thousands of years. Part of what makes this region's ancient forests feel so special is that they have largely been left intact as primeval ecosystems undisturbed by human activity.

Today, when you stand at the base of an enormous tree, it's difficult to process the destruction wrought by the logging industry in the original redwood forests of Northern California. Early twentieth-century prospectors seeking gold recognized the trees held great value, and improving technology made harvesting more efficient. Old-growth forests were cleared at a rapid rate as Humboldt County and the surrounding region quickly evolved to support this new population of laborers and the infrastructure of farms, roads, and towns they needed. In fact, two-thirds of the 120,000 forested acres now protected in Redwood National and State Parks were clear-cut before the parks' establishment, and commercial logging went on outside the parks through the 1990s, leaving only four percent of the original forests of the region. Much of what we see today are second-growth redwood forests, planted after clear-cutting. You can feel the difference between an old-growth forest and a second-growth forest—in the latter, the trees are more tightly packed and, though still large, are noticeably smaller. In old growth, the trunks are farther apart.

Vicki Ozaki, a retired geologist with the National Park Service, walked with us through Prairie Creek Redwoods State Park and explained that although logging wreaked havoc on the watershed, ecosystem restoration work is going on full steam ahead as part of Redwoods Rising, a joint effort of California State Parks, the National Park Service, and Save the Redwoods League. The first step is to thin the dense second-growth redwood trees. Each year after this thinning, all the roads in the area have to be "pulled" (removed), starting at the top of the watershed and working outward. Many logging roads, she explained, were put in before California had its current Forest Practice Rules, leading to significant damage to hillslopes and streams. Vicki acknowledged that it's not possible to treat every area due to the massive scale of disturbance and funding limitations, so the restoration work aims to tackle areas that will create a connection between blocks of old growth.

Today, the redwood forests' biggest threats include climate change, fire, illegal marijuana farms, and yes, believe it or not, clear-cutting that still occurs as forests are converted to farms, homes, and vineyards. Without the dedicated effort of people literally laying their bodies on the line and speaking for the trees, the redwood forests we're able to visit today would not be here. The spirit of these activists lives on through the myriad nonprofits that continue to serve as guardians of these majestic forests.

• ✦ •

For us, like most people, coming to the redwoods conjured up images of massive trees in dense forests. It hadn't occurred to us until we arrived that an essential part of the redwoods story is actually the *ocean*. In fact, the North Coast redwoods could not exist without it.

The Pacific Ocean serves as climate control for the redwood forests just a few miles inland. The coastal effect means it's neither too hot and dry nor too cold, and the cool ocean air produces the fog that redwoods use as a water source. You can see how these trees drink up this moisture in the needlelike redwood leaves that flutter to the forest floor. "Sun foliage" from the lower branches, as one volunteer ranger explained to us, is flat and neat, whereas "fog foliage" from the top of the canopy is notably more wispy, evolved to drink moisture from the fog rolling in off the ocean.

As we traveled the coast, we learned more about the interdependency between the redwood forests and the ocean, like how beaches, dunes, cliffs, and coastal trees such as Sitka spruce and white alder create a buffer between the harsh winds and salt water from the ocean and the redwood forests. In turn, the redwoods provide shade that keeps the water cool, and they prevent erosion along alluvial floodplains by holding sediment. Logging threw off the balance of this complex ecosystem, eroding soil and spawning mudslides that buried rivers and streams; the disturbance and removal of fallen logs erased vital wildlife habitat and altered the force and flow of water—all of which decimated wildlife dependent on the forests and riparian habitats, including Pacific salmon.

Many of the region's largest and oldest trees are found near creeks exposed to flooding and silting. These environments protect the trees from wind and provide them with ample water and nutrients to grow. In turn, redwoods that have fallen into the streams slow the flow of water to create calm pools where juvenile fish can seek refuge. These waterways are home to river otters; coho and Chinook (king) salmon; steelhead and coastal cutthroat trout; and lamprey—making them important feeding grounds not only for the people who live along them but also for the marine life where these rivers drain into the ocean. When salmon swim upstream to spawn in freshwater, they release their eggs and die, and their rotting bodies put nutrients back into the streams, feeding the redwood trees. Once in abundance in the region's rivers and their tributaries, salmon and steelhead trout populations have been drastically reduced by logging. Now many local, state, and tribal agencies and fisheries work in partnership to restore their populations.

The interplay between coast and redwoods creates habitat for other forms of wildlife as well. One of the most fascinating stories we heard on the Redwood Coast was about the marbled murrelet, a bird related to seabirds like puffins and murres, which typically nest on cliffs or sea stacks along the coast. Until the 1970s, marbled murrelet nesting behaviors were a mystery—that is, until a worker trimming storm-damaged branches at Big Basin Redwoods State Park discovered a marbled murrelet chick 150 feet up on a mossy branch. Through evolutionary adaptation, this seabird has become a forest bird.

• ✦ •

Many locals enjoyed casually unfurling the phrase "behind the Redwood Curtain" in conversation with us, but its meaning was often elusive. For some, it's a point of pride for the unique community tucked away behind a wall of majestic redwood forests; being "behind the curtain" together fosters self-reliance, a sense of identity, and a feeling of community, and reinforces the choice of many here to disconnect from the rest of the world.

For others, the curtain encapsulates a sense of isolation created by geography or dreary weather. Sometimes landslides or downed trees leave them cut off from main routes. While the Redwood Coast continues to attract residents and visitors for its stunning forests, sweeping coastal beaches, and charming small towns, this access to beauty doesn't come without the extremes and risks often found in wild places. For starters, the same fog that delivers water to the redwoods also casts a gray gloom over the coast. The region is also prone to seismic activity due to its location on top of the Cascadia subduction zone and proximity to the Mendocino Triple Junction, a point where three tectonic plates meet. Earthquakes on land or offshore can trigger tsunamis. In 1964, a series of five waves set off by an earthquake in Alaska hit Crescent City in a devastating tsunami that killed a number of residents and wiped out its downtown, destroying 29 city blocks and more than 289 buildings and homes.

For many, "behind the Redwood Curtain" also evokes a painful—and not-too-distant—hidden history. This traces back to the acculturation, discrimination, racism, and a violent history of expulsion and murder that people have faced here. To collect stories that accurately represent this place, we knew we had to look past the allure of the majestic forests to understand the history of human occupation. As with many other natural areas in North America, behind this complex landscape is also a complex human history.

For thousands of years, Indigenous people stewarded these lands that we now enjoy, and Chinese immigrants built the roads that enable us to travel here. In Muir Woods, ranger Mia Monroe explained that the visitor center exhibits once told only the story of how, in 1903, Elizabeth and William Kent, wealthy and well-known figures in Marin County, bought the land that is now the national monument. They donated it to the government in order to preserve it, asking that it be named after their inspiring friend John Muir. "We told this story because it's true," Mia said, "and also because we wanted everyone to realize that there's something *everyone* can do, big or small. But it left out ten thousand years of Miwok people that were stewarding the land. It left out all the women's garden clubs that Elizabeth was part of who were really the movers and shakers behind those famous guys. It really left out that William Kent was a racist.... You know, it left out a lot of things." While the Kents' legacy of conservation efforts is enduring, it's also important to recognize that William fought to exclude Japanese and Chinese immigrants throughout his three terms in the US House of Representatives (1911 to 1917).

We also cannot overlook the greed of white settlers scrambling for gold after its discovery in the Klamath, Trinity, and Salmon Rivers in 1849, which resulted in the violent removal, expulsion, and genocide of Native peoples. For tens of thousands of years, Indigenous tribes—predominantly the Chilula, Karuk, Hupa, Tolowa, Wiyot, and Yurok—lived in balance with the land. Tribes maintained their own laws and customs, and often intermarried and participated in each other's ceremonies. Living in small groups, Native peoples often established permanent settlements near food and water sources, with a few dozen redwood plank houses built into the ground, their roofs peeking out aboveground with openings just big enough for humans and too small for the once-native grizzlies. Through hunting and gathering, they subsisted on the bounty of the region: tanoak acorns, deer, elk, salmon, steelhead, and other river fish. Even today, many of the tribes prepare for the fall salmon runs with ceremonies, fish camps, and other social gatherings.

When European settlers arrived, Native tribes were forced to relocate to reservations or remote areas, ceding tribal lands, or assimilate into American society. The small tracts of land that the US government offered displaced Northern California tribes were called rancherías instead of reservations, a nod to the history of Spanish settlement. After decades of broken treaties and terminations, Indigenous advocates gained enough traction to establish many of the remaining rancherías as federally recognized tribal entities, with rights to self-governance and access to resources and services. Many Indigenous people from the local tribes still live in the region and remain active members of the community and stewards of this land. More than thirty of the tribes operate casinos on their land with the promise of economic independence.

It wasn't only Indigenous people who faced expulsion and discrimination among the redwoods. In the mid-1800s, Chinese immigrants labored in the mines and lumber mills, and on the roads and railroads, but there was a backlash against them. Vicki Ozaki, who is not only a retired geologist but also one of the organizers of Humboldt Asians and Pacific Islanders in Solidarity (HAPI), described to us how Chinese residents had built a vibrant Chinatown in newly booming Eureka, California, where they worked in salmon canneries, laundries, farms, fisheries, and restaurants. White residents were threatened by Chinese laborers' willingness to work longer hours for lower pay, and by their different culture, religion, and language, which kept the Chinese community from assimilating. This brewing xenophobia came to a head on February 6, 1885, when a Eureka city councilman was killed by a stray bullet from crossfire between Chinese residents. A quickly formed committee ruled that all Chinese residents had twenty-four hours to leave town, and it put them on steamships headed to San Francisco. This "Eureka method" became a model for other expulsions across California. At one point, Humboldt County even advertised itself in its business directory as "the only county in the state containing no Chinamen."

In spite of this ugly history, in many ways Northern California has now become a model for what facing our past and shaping our future could look like. After two centuries of displacement, genocide, and restricted access to their traditional lands, Indigenous tribes in Northern California are collaborating with parks and state agencies in the management, renewal, and restoration of Native lands. Renewal of the forests is critical for the preservation of their culture and the land sacred to them, as well as the entirety of our planet and in combating our collective biggest threat: the climate crisis. As one of our contributors, Shaunna McCovey, writes in her piece, tribes are "working with the Parks to find common ground in the middle of our differences."

On the California State Parks side, we spoke to Victor Bjelajac, superintendent of the North Coast Redwoods District, who acknowledged that the 280 parks he oversees are located on the ancestral territories of Indigenous tribes. "Because of historical and contemporary wrongs, state parks on California's North Coast have been trying to right some of the actions that have kept Indigenous peoples from accessing and being in relationship with homelands now managed through a Western cultural lens. We do this by developing relationships with Indigenous peoples of the area, listening to their needs and aspirations, and by welcoming them home to practice their lifeways on their ancestral lands."

In the past, state rules and regulations about gathering natural resources, intended to prevent overextraction and protect fragile coastal ecosystems, have created barriers for Indigenous people wanting to harvest materials for ceremony, basketry, and plant medicines. Today, policies prejudiced against California's Native tribes are being updated and reshaped in collaborations between state and tribal governments. In 2022, California State Parks and the Yurok Tribe signed a historic traditional tribal gathering agreement that allows anyone with a tribal identification card to gather plants and minerals within state parks inside of the North Coast Redwoods District and within Yurok ancestral territory, as well as participate in tribal activities for religious, spiritual, ceremonial, recreational, and research purposes.

California State Parks is also taking a fresh and critical look at its past—rethinking, updating, removing, and changing place names, monuments, and interpretive signage and information. Much of this work is done in consultation and partnership with Indigenous tribes and has led to meaningful and significant changes, such as the renaming of Patrick's Point State Park (named for a homesteader who was implicated in the murder of a Native American boy and led a militia that massacred a Native American village) to Sue-meg State Park and the installation of land acknowledgment signs throughout North Coast Redwoods District parks.

And in Eureka, celebration of the town's missing Chinese history and culture is coming back to its streets thanks to HAPI, which has hosted a series of performances to foster dialogue and convey lessons on civil rights and resilience. In 2021, HAPI worked with the descendants of Charlie Moon, one of the few Chinese Americans who was able to evade the 1885 expulsion, to get an alley designated Charlie Moon Way, anchoring historic Eureka Chinatown. HAPI's Eureka Chinatown Project has raised funds from donations and grants to create a monument that honors the residents of the former enclave, give voice to those silenced and erased by expulsion, help people understand this part of Humboldt County's history, and imagine a future of communities living together.

One of the goals of *Campfire Stories* is to surface narratives that have been forgotten or left out. We are moved by the Native and Asian American communities of the Redwood Coast and how they embody the spirit of repair, restoration, and resilience we also see exemplified in the recovery of the redwood forests. We are left feeling hopeful as we witness historical memorials dedicated to problematic figures being removed, interpretive signs with incomplete narratives being revised or replaced, names of parks and landmarks changing to reflect Indigenous place names, and land acknowledgments being added.

• ✦ •

When we weren't hiking the redwood forests in pouring rain, looking out over the Pacific from the coastal cliffs, or immersing ourselves in the region's rich natural and cultural landmarks, we were inside libraries, archives, and bookstores—interviewing locals to help us identify themes and stories for this collection. We talked with countless individuals who live and work on the North Coast about the most meaningful writers and works to come from this corner of the world, as well as gathering practical tips on where to go, what to do, where to camp, and perhaps most important, how to visit in ways that respect and support these communities and places. It is our hope that these tips from locals, combined with our own experiences, contextualize the stories within and offer guidance if you do visit one day.

These stories are meant to be read around a "fire," whether quietly to yourself from the comfort of your couch or aloud to the people sharing the ember glow of a campfire with you. These are not stories for those seeking just to be entertained with classic spooky stories, but were collected instead for those who are curious about how this special region came to be and why it continues to mean so much to us—because the stories we tell shape our values and our future.

Our time on the North Coast taught us that the true value of the redwoods lies not only in the region's beauty and majesty but even more in what it teaches us about resilience and survival. The trees' perseverance through thousands of years of forest fires, temperature changes, floods, and drought, and how they regenerate from injury through burls and roots, means that their rings read not just as a history book but also as an instruction manual in tenacity and restoration. Dan Sealy, a retired National Park Service ranger and legislative analyst with the Northcoast Environmental Center who hosted us during our stay, said it's important to remember that "when we make a mistake, nature is pretty strong. If we do the right thing, we can actually fix what we screw up." The Redwood Coast shows us what can happen when we pull back the curtain enough to let the light in—to expose difficult truths, learn from mistakes, and work collectively toward repair.

Whether you've visited a hundred times or only through the pages of this book, we hope this collection deepens your connection to this majestic place. We hope you enjoy these stories from past and present as much as we do, and that you find yourself, or your sense of the wild, in these words.

Storytelling Tips

Storytelling has always been a fundamental part of being human. Beyond entertainment, stories have allowed us to share knowledge, traditions, and ideas, and to feel a sense of connection with people and places beyond our own experiences for thousands of years.

Through all its forms, we have witnessed how stories can create deeper emotional connections between people and the natural world. This is especially true across generations and communities who have been disconnected from the outdoors, yet who are, increasingly, responsible for protecting it.

We believe that stories are best when they're shared with others, so we encourage you to share any stories or sections you love with friends or family, continuing in the tradition of oral storytelling, by sharing them aloud.

Should you find yourself gathered with others around a campfire, here are some tips for sharing a story:

Be prepared. A campfire can provide a warm, flickering light that sets the perfect mood but may not be adequate for reading a book, so bring a lantern, flashlight, headlamp, or book light. A glass of water can rescue you from a fit of coughing or a dry mouth, so keep it handy. In a camp setting with crickets and a crackling fire, you may be competing to be heard—sit or stand up straight, breathe from your diaphragm, and project your voice.

Choose the right story. Choose a story that matches your audience's interests, age, attention span, and the moment. Pay attention to length; if it's too long, consider summarizing and read aloud only a particularly interesting or engaging poem or passage.

Introduce the story. Explain why you want to read this story, what it's about, and who wrote it—keeping it short and sweet. (Feel free to use our insider knowledge from the "About This Story" sections to get your audience excited.) End with a thought about what you took away from it and a question to engage your listeners.

Bring the story alive. Every story, especially poetry, has its own rhythm. When you read aloud, read it slightly faster than you would naturally speak but without rushing. Keep your listeners' attention by breaking up the rhythm with a long pause or a different cadence. (But don't overuse this trick or overperform!) Be authentic, enunciate clearly, and let your natural reactions enhance the story without disrupting the flow.

Most of all, have fun! Whether reading this book around a campfire, in your living room, at a park, or tucked cozily in bed, we hope you will find something that makes the natural world come alive.

Beyond the Great Divide of the West
And far into the setting sun,
There is a land of primeval beauty,
Of clean towering strength . . .
A Land of the Giants.

Here it is
That long lines of marching mountains
Bar the crashing waves of the ocean;
And sleeping sands with sentinel rocks
Break the deep breathings of a restless sea . . .

—BERNICE RIDLEY,
MEMORIES FROM HUMBOLDT (1956)

REDWOOD COAST

STORIES

California's Giant Trees

HARRIETT E. WEAVER

Excerpts from *Adventures in the Redwoods*

California's giant redwoods are renowned everywhere on earth, and rightfully so. Where else but in the coastal forests can you stand in a shadowy world of stillness and tranquility and let your gaze wander up a living shaft to a canopy of green foliage often hidden by clouds and drifting fog? Where else but in the high mountains a hundred miles inland from there must twenty to thirty people have to clasp hands before they can encircle a red trunk massive enough to plug up a city street?

Of three known types of redwoods, two grow in California and one of them lops over a bit into Oregon. That redwood, the tall coastal tree, inhabits nine counties along the sea and is scientifically classified as *Sequoia sempervirens* or Coast redwood—or just plain redwood for short. The bulky Sierra redwood, found in six Sierra Nevada counties, is classified *Sequoiadendron giganteum*—too much of a mouthful to be bandied about lightly. We call it the Sequoia or Big Tree. And so it shall be in this book.

To visit the third member of the relationship, the Metasequoia (new sequoia) or Dawn redwood, you would have to trudge into remote China. Anyway, since this redwood rises a mere hundred feet, is bare-stemmed in winter, and was thought to have been extinct for twenty million years, it wouldn't intrigue you like California's own except as a living fossil, which it truly is.

The story of the giant redwood goes back into antiquity a hundred million years to a time when much of the planet was covered with warm seas, when some of its creatures were deserting water for dry land and monstrous reptiles dominated all living things. Nowhere as yet were there any broadleaf trees or flowering plants, but towering above the ungainly dinosaurs were conifers so enormous that they dwarfed the mightiest of prehistoric beasts. It was of such a time and place that the redwoods' fight for survival began.

With the passing of long epochs, earthquakes buckled and shifted entire continents and ocean basins. Volcanoes spewed lava over vast areas. The sun scorched and withered, and dried up the surface waters. Unable to cope with such cataclysms, the dinosaurs and their kind vanished from the scene, but the big trees that had fed and sheltered them somehow carried forward their own thread of life. And scarcely changing form, this thread has endured through the ages; down through thousands and thousands of centuries of mountain building and extremes of climate.

About 60 million years ago, predecessors of the big redwoods we know today flourished over much of the Northern Hemisphere. Their fossil remains have been discovered among the bones and footprints of dinosaurs, in England, Switzerland, Norway, France, Germany, Austria, Japan, Central Asia, and parts of the United States. It boggles the mind to contemplate how their seeds, together with the migrating animals, crossed the land connection between Siberia and Alaska. On Saint Lawrence Island in the Bering Sea, where now no trees at all can grow, fossil evidence shows that both redwoods and their present companions, the oaks, alders, and maples once existed there. At the same time, Greenland was living up to its name, hosting a luxurious growth. This was before extensive land uplift changed the tropical climate, for even though the Appalachians were then hills thousands of years old, and the Sierra Nevada was forming, the Andes, Alps, Himalayas, and Rockies had not yet risen.

The redwoods, however, were not destined to occupy all their original wide-ranging domain. A million or two years ago advancing ice sheets crowded them into a last stand in California and Southwest Oregon. Along the coast, the retreating glaciers left behind a fairly continuous belt of redwoods about 500 miles long ranging today from below Big Sur, south of Monterey, to a few miles above the California-Oregon border. Always just out of reach of the wind-blown spray, the trees inhabit sheltered, well-watered places of rich soil as far inland as the fog drifts—20 miles or more—and up the Coast Range mountainsides to about 3000 feet—or until good soil, sufficient moisture and suitable slopes give out. Their forests are vast, dark, dense, and understandably lush with an infinite variety of underbrush because of the 80 to 140-inch annual rainfall. Thus, the groves of really magnificent giants stand on riverside flats, where winter floods supplement the lifegiving downpour and provide layers of nutritious sediment as well. And when the winter rains finally wind up for the year, usually in April, often in May, wet summer fogs hover over the forests and slow the sun's evaporation of precious moisture. . . .

• ✦ •

The coast redwoods seem to meld into an atmosphere of reverence akin to that found in a great cathedral—only this cathedral is not of stone but of living walls, softly mauve. Its ceiling is not of hand-carved rafters but of open sky; its windows not of stained glass but of lacy foliage high above, through which the sun filters in golden shafts. . . .

• ✦ •

By actual ring count, the oldest known Coast redwood has lived 2,200 years. It is only 12 feet in diameter, not nearly as large as countless others much younger that have grown up under more favorable conditions. It was felled in 1934 in the Avenue of the Giants, Humboldt County, in a very dense forest, so it never did attain the height and bulk it might have, had abundant sunlight been available. Most Coast redwoods measure 10 to 12 feet in diameter, some up to 18 or more feet and are as much as 60 feet around. One of the largest known, the Santa Clara Tree in Big Basin Redwoods State Park, measures 17 feet 9 inches at breast height (4½ feet above the ground and root swell) and 55 feet in circumference. Rising straight and impressive, the Santa Clara tapers so little that at 100 feet it is still 40 feet around—not massive like some of the monstrous Big Trees in the Sierra, but nevertheless a giant to behold among the slenderer coast trees. . . .

• ✦ •

For years, the 364-foot Founders Tree at Dyerville Flats in the Redwood Empire topped all living things. Then a storm whacked off the tip. A few years later, some towering 368-foot trees were discovered on private lands in an area on Redwood Creek east of Orick, now a part of the Redwood National Park. The new champions may in turn be challenged anytime some intrepid explorer finds a taller tree, or if lightning bolts and hurricane-force winds tear off their lofty crowns, or if falling neighbors expose a tree to full sunlight, releasing it to head for the open sky at 3 feet a year.

Together, the coastal giants form a skyscraping forest. As they grow older and rise higher and higher, and after their crowns have merged into a dark canopy that permits almost no passage of sunlight, they drop their lower limbs, laying bare their trunks a long way up.

The volume of board footage contained in such trees is difficult to grasp. For our imaginations to be stirred, we have to compare the immense timber volume with familiar things. Men with slide rules and an eye for construction can tell that twenty 5-room cottages could be built from the Santa Clara Tree (Heaven forbid), or, from even larger redwoods, a school of a hundred class rooms with enough left over for an auditorium. In like terms, the General Sherman could be spoken of as forty 5-room cottages, or, as has been stated by park naturalists, a crate large enough to house the Queen Mary.

One might imagine that anything as tall and slender as a coast redwood must surely be anchored near the center of the earth. Not so. Not so the sequoia either. Supporting all that spectacular bulk and weight is a remarkable balance, poised precariously on a pocket of roots so shallow as to defy belief. The root pad extends downward only 6 or 8 feet, although the network of small feeder roots may spread over several acres. The coast redwoods root themselves only 4 to 6 feet down, and their feeder roots, some hair-fine and just inches beneath the forest floor litter, reach out only one or two hundred feet, entwining with the roots of their neighbors. Neither type of redwood has a taproot to ram its way far below and act as a groundgripper, holding the columns solidly erect through the centuries. Nothing continues to burrow deeper and deeper into the mother soil as the trees rise higher and higher above it. The only really strong anchorage both giants have is surface roots. Like great claws they clutch the ground at the base. But even so, these sometimes fail to save a tall willowy redwood from toppling in the furious winds off the sea that whip the tree tops back and forth. Even when the roots hold, the trunks creak and groan, and huge limbs crash to the ground. These are called "Widowmakers" by rangers and their wives for a reason easy to guess.

Along with such storms, erosion is the redwoods worst natural enemy. Every year many fall as floodwaters tear away the soil around their roots and slipping mountainsides bulldoze them over. Giants come crashing down, and when they do, the earth shakes. Even the largest of trees are carried away by the water, some clear to the sea, where they litter the beaches.

Others may not drop completely but simply lean, possibly because a section of their root systems has been killed by fire, or some of their neighbors, in falling, have forced them off kilter. To save themselves, the leaners ingeniously redistribute the weight of their trunks by widening the growth rings on the weak side while narrowing and sometimes discontinuing them on the opposite side, thereby building a buttress of wood. The longer the giant stands, the larger and sturdier the buttress becomes, forming what is known as a flatiron tree. With this support, it may survive longer than redwoods that have always stood straight and undisturbed. . . .

• ✦ •

After you see lightning zigzag across the sky or watch on television flames roaring through thousands of acres of forestlands, you may wonder why the long-lived redwoods are not consumed like all the other trees. The answer is that the great trees are protected by multiple defenses that guard them against fire, disease, and decay.

Their first line of defense against fire is a soft pithy bark—on the coast redwoods a foot or less thick, on the sequoias up to 3 feet through, and so asbestos-like as to be virtually fireproof.

The bark contains no pitch or resin, the sticky substance that causes trees like pines and firs to flare up in such a hurry. In addition, the wood beneath the bark contains a great deal of water, which slows burning even when a blaze manages to gain entrance through a break in the bark. The great blackened caverns, so often found in the base of big old giants, were probably the work of not one but a series of holocausts over a long period of time. Such wildfires usually destroy the rest of the forest, including young redwoods that have not yet had time to mature and develop thick hides.

Not only does the bark save the trees from fire; it protects them against heat and cold as well. Even should the interior be blazing fiercely, the bark would still be cool to the touch.

Sometimes lightning plays havoc with the treetops, setting crown fires and shattering limbs, but the electricity will not be carried downward via the bark because it is a nonconductor. Attempts to force as much as 5000 volts through it have failed. Small wonder that redwood bark is considered an excellent insulating material.

In any forest, falling trees usually strike and injure others. After such an occurrence or a fire, a redwood's "growing" part gets busy and does some healing work. This is the thin cambium layer just beneath the bark that widens the tree by one ring each year. Eventually, it forms a new skin that closes the wound, much as human flesh responds to a similar need. Other trees aren't long-lived enough to heal their injuries; but a giant has all the time in the world—with luck, many centuries. And so effective can its coverup be that no one would ever suspect that there is a great charred hole sealed off from view inside that huge trunk. In time, scar tissue and even outer bark will have completely obliterated all trace. Only after the giant is down and a cross-section taken, will the truth be discovered. . . .

The burned-out heartwood is the giants' first and oldest growth and is dead tissue, so its loss is not a devastating one. What's important is the living tissue, the cream-colored sapwood surrounding it that conducts water and minerals from the roots up to the leaves, where they are converted into food, and the inner bark that carries nutrients downward to supply the whole tree. After a fire, if enough of the sapwood remains in contact with the earth to pull sufficient moisture as high as the crown, the vigorous and healthy foliage and cones will be ample evidence of continuing life. If not, the top may die. Most of the "spiketops" seen on the forest skyline are the result of fire damage; the rest have been caused by lightning strikes and wind damage.

In addition to the thick, fire-resistant bark, the trees are further protected by special chemicals—principally tannin. You can see it in the vivid coloring of both bark and heartwood and sometimes as a dark stain flowing over raw broken surfaces, creosoting them against the ravages of time and the invasion of insects and disease, which occurs when a tree fractures in crashing to the ground and is left there.

Almost all fallen trees decay rather rapidly—but not redwoods. Thanks to their tannin, even giants that have lain partially buried for centuries are in good enough condition to be hauled away to the mill and sawed into lumber, the same as standing trees.

Redwoods are sometimes attacked by insects and fungi but almost never damaged seriously, thanks again to tannin. Fungi, unable to manufacture food themselves, must live off some other substance. In doing so, they cause the dead tissues to decay and often kill the living. A brown heart rot, for instance, in gaining entry through the bark or a burn, will in time eat into the heartwood; and while not destroying the tree, it nevertheless ruins the wood and creates a natural fuel that when ignited, will smolder internally for weeks or months.

Most trees are subject to injury and death by some kind of insect, and the redwood is not totally immune. It has to fight off a tiny insect that tends to reduce the bark just under the surface to a powder, although not endangering the tree. And while the sapwood isn't necessarily immune to termites, lumber cut from the tannin-rich heartwood will resist their attacks for countless years, even in the high humidity of the tropics where they continuously reduce wood construction and jungle growth to humus. One thing is certain: redwood lumber will be sturdy and useful long after other woods have crumbled into dust.

Although a redwood tree can survive a series of raging forest fires and resist infection and decay, it is no match for its worst enemy—man.

With travel and visitation to the giants increasing year after year, the soil around the base of the trees is becoming so trampled and compacted that the feeder roots are crushed and the flow of water and nutrients up through the trunks to the crowns is blocked. The bark of the surface roots becomes so gashed and bruised by people climbing over them to have their pictures taken, that barriers have had to be erected to restrain the hordes of sightseers. Understandably, the park services have had to limit automobile access, and new construction, and even camping under the big trees. This policy applies in many groves of both coast and Sierra, where some roads have been closed to traffic and entire beaten-up areas gradually fenced off and "put to bed" for years, to rest and recover from man's over-enthusiastic attentions. This way, winters will loosen the soil and the nutritious ground litter will remain undisturbed for a long time. Hopefully, the crowns of the giants will then stop turning brown, and begin regaining their healthy green. The forest floor, once more rich in nutrients, will become soft and springy. Small plants and flowers of all kinds will reappear, as very slowly the forest recovers from "people erosion."

The next time you return to your favorite redwood park and find your oldtime campsite closed, be patient and understanding. It is resting and rejuvenating so your grandchildren and theirs will have these same giants to enjoy, just as you and your children have.

About This Story

Born in 1908, Harriett Eiline "Petey" Weaver lived a life of many careers. She taught school in Southern California for thirty-five years, spent twenty-one summers as the first female ranger in the California state parks (fourteen of those in Big Basin Redwoods State Park), and wrote ten books, three of them about redwoods. Her first two redwoods books were published by iconic California publisher Sunset Books, and she served for many years as an editorial consultant there. After the publication and success of her own books, Petey was asked to write a teaching unit on redwoods published by the California Redwood Association.

Her calling card was the knowledge and enthusiasm that imbue her essay. She earned her nickname after high school classmates shortened her baseball moniker from PDQ (Pretty Darn Quick) to just PD, and then Petey. In 1971, the California State Park Rangers Association selected Petey as an honorary ranger, celebrating her exemplary contribution to California state parks. After she passed away in 1993, a coast redwood tree was dedicated in her memory at Humboldt Redwoods State Park, and her autobiography, *Me and the Mother Tree*, was published by the California State Park Rangers Association.

In addition to providing a great overview of the organisms that make up the redwood forest, Petey captures the essential contradiction of the redwoods. While we admire their longevity—made possible by their resistance to fire, infection, and decay; and their ability to heal and regenerate—we also threaten their survival by heedlessly tromping around on their shallow root systems. Petey implores readers to be patient and understanding, and to join her in the project of protecting these ancient, giant trees.

Restoration

HEATHER BOURBEAU

Muir Woods

As an avid hiker who lives in the Bay Area, I often seek redwoods. But when I need to be fully immersed and humbled, I specifically head for Muir Woods. I long for mycorrhizal networks, tree roots and fungi spreading, speaking to each other, showing the beauty of communal salvation.

When I hike into Muir Woods, I take the back trails not because I cannot or do not want to pay or park. I hike miles into these woods because it is a more meditative entrance into the majestic groves, because I can descend silently, nearly alone, in the fog among younger redwoods and because in this descent, my breath deepens and my thoughts of the future or the past are stilled momentarily. I pet the furlike bark, bend my head to meet tree trunks, share breath and thanks.

I know that once I reach Redwood Creek and the official demarcation of the park, I will hear voices, be pulled into the human. Encouraged silence in Cathedral Grove will force us to be present with these woods that are quietly saving us, but it is hard to not ask of a companion, "Isn't this magical?" And so many people do. I will fight my urge to hold onto quietude just a bit longer before I hear testimony and awe in many languages. The sound of water running over rocks. Soft cover of needle and bay leaves. Fern and redwood sorrel, tanoak and thimbleberry. Fallen. Fodder.

A friend's daughter in Germany was obsessed with the idea of redwoods when she was nine. When they came for a visit, I wanted to share my hike into Muir Woods, but she wasn't too excited for the five-mile trek. And so we walked one of my favorite trails within the park and stopped to admire one very large tree. She paused, then asked, "Is that all?" The adults laughed and immediately held hands and tried (and failed) to encircle the trunk to show how massive the tree was. While the rest of us were marveling at the height, the width, the age of this organism, the daughter remained only slightly moved. We asked, "See how big this is? Isn't it amazing?" She responded, "I thought they could reach the moon!" The extraordinary power of a child's imagination. Perhaps, I thought, we adults can dream that big again. Perhaps, these trees can grow taller. Perhaps, if we get out of the way, if we imagine the interconnectedness under and over us, another kind of magic can manifest.

Ten years later, my friend's daughter returned as a young adult with her best friend. She wanted to revisit the trees she loved so well, to see them through her older eyes. This time, we camped near the western peak of Mount Tamalpais and hiked my favorite back trail into Muir Woods. Five miles, several bridges, two campgrounds, a meadow, the songs of several birds, the scent of leaves warming in the sun. We descended into the flatter creek bed before the park; fungi and lichen and moss signaled our approach. Sweat cooling, our pulses slowed, our hearts opened.

When we reached Redwood Creek, full and flowing, we noticed a man staring intently into the water. A local, he was transfixed, smiling. In response, I motioned to the girls for silence and saw, as tears came to my eyes, the coho. Fat and large and moving upstream. The coho is near extinction in this creek. Coho salmon numbers along the central California coast are estimated to be 1 percent of their historic levels, which does not bode well for Muir Woods. Coho are a keystone species, meaning they are essential to a healthy ecosystem. When their populations decline or disappear, there are massive repercussions. We know this now. Almost too late. Almost. But not quite.

Juvenile coho need shelter, roots and rocks, pools and bends to cover and survive. In the 1930s, in the height of the Depression, the Civilian Conservation Corps (CCC) employed mostly young men to help in public lands, forests, and parks in the United States. Between 1934 and 1938, CCC crews hauled in boulders and lined them along 3,300 feet of Redwood Creek to theoretically prevent erosion. Control in the guise of conservation. They also cleared large areas of understory so that visitors could have better views of the tallest trees. The coho born in Redwood Creek in Muir Woods became much less likely to survive than those from farther downstream.

Less than ten years later, the nonprofit Save the Redwoods League proposed the secretary of the interior invite the US president and more than five hundred delegates from forty-six nations to come to Muir Woods during their San Francisco–based conference to create a United Nations. The secretary argued that Muir Woods was "a temple of peace" that could offer much-needed perspective. The delegates gathered quietly in the Cathedral Grove and paid tribute to President Roosevelt, who had recently died. US Secretary of State Edward R. Stettinius, Jr., closed out the ceremony, saying, "These great redwoods at Muir Woods National Monument are the most enduring of all trees," and pointing out that many of them would stand for "centuries after every man now living is dead." He did not understand that the recent efforts to clear and carve had put in danger not only the trees but also everything around them.

A multiyear restoration project is now bringing back habitat for not only the coho but also the steelhead trout and California red-legged frogs. Nitrogen from salmon that have successfully spawned feeds the trees. This interconnectedness is not abstract. The removal of the riprap and planting of new growth along the creek bed has allowed not only the coho to thrive but also insects and plants and other wildlife that lead to a healthier and more sustainable ecosystem. Young salamanders, scarlet monkey flowers, water striders, horsetails, dragonflies, and tiger swallowtails have also returned.

When I saw that coho with my German friend, my hands instinctively went to my heart, then a silent, mimed applause. The man who pointed it out to me and I nearly hugged. Two years after creek restoration work had begun, the salmon were coming back. We were in a joy our visitors could not exactly understand, as they had not lived through our droughts and uncontrolled fires and habitat losses. But they understood they were witnessing something extraordinary. And when I pointed out the tree she had once dismissed as not tall enough, she leaned in and laughed at her younger self. As we hiked out, she paused again before the creek, noticed dragonflies, waited for another salmon.

Today, I hike in thick fog, notice fresh redwood starts with bright green needles. There are flags to mark recent plantings. Boughs and fern fronds, bay leaves and broken branches. California spikenard grows along the trail, brown creepers sing overhead, an adolescent deer with fuzz for horns. Here is the proof of what we can do when we pause together, quiet the need to control, listen to the land, undo damage done in the name of preservation. Thick trunks, moisture held, river runs. Restoration, redemption. Hope.

About This Story

Poet and writer Heather Bourbeau grew up visiting the redwoods along the California and Oregon coasts. Now living within walking distance of regional parks that celebrate redwoods and serving as a docent at Point Reyes National Seashore, Bourbeau finds that the redwoods and their larger ecology permeate her poetry and fiction. Write what you know, the saying goes, and Bourbeau knows the redwoods.

In addition to telling some of the foundational stories of restoration and redemption that we heard in Muir Woods in her piece, Bourbeau shares the route commonly used by locals who are seeking a more "meditative" approach to the park and these famous trees. Another writer in this collection, John Hart, shared with us that if you want to beat the crowds at Muir, consider the "spectacular" stand of redwood trees at Steep Ravine in Mount Tamalpais State Park, which adjoins Muir Woods and was given to the State of California by the same donor who gave Muir Woods to the nation. Whether among the crowds or on your own, it's a balm to be in the presence of the symbols of hope and restoration that lie within these woods.

Redwood Forest

JOHN HART

And in some canyon, angled from the sun,
with a little fence around it, and a sign,
is a cool place
where the necessity of things
works itself up in leaves.

Time slowed as in that Einstein clock
they showed us, to imagine, in a book,
the splendid heartwood wastefully alive,
the great forms rising, half-intelligent,
and hung with those unhinged light-seeking things.

We call this grove memorial.
To our own veterans, we mean.
It shadows us with its surcease of green.
And we come clicking at the mighty vegetables,
exclaiming at the tall stabilities,
things seen and subtle, and the subtler things not seen.

In shade we wander, ignorant and chattering, though knowing
more than these
of what decays.
They charm us with our littleness.
And we infest them, tiny, dangerous,
the misty, tricky, changeable, unfilled.
Our very tread more death to them than fire.

We who have carved in every kind of wood
the separation and the grief of god—
we who have pulled the rotten forests down—
come now to wonder at and praise
the manumission that let this one live.

As if this grove could speak for us somehow
before some tribunal of green and mournful things
(the long mantis faces dubious):
as if we could say to the Angel: Sister: See:
we didn't destroy it all.

About This Story

We came across environmental journalist and poet John Hart's books on Muir Woods while we were researching this collection, and asked if he'd be open to meeting us for coffee. We met at the Depot Café and Bookstore, considered the heart of Mill Valley, a small town adjacent to Muir Woods with homes woven between redwoods and a downtown with boutique shops and a vibrant art scene. The cafe was buzzing with activity—customers picking up weekend reads, whole families riding in on cargo bikes, and friends dining on sandwiches with cocktails and coffee. John, who ordered his coffee black, is a soft-spoken man who we at times had to lean in closer to hear over the live band playing in the large back patio.

When we asked him how he ended up writing his book *Muir Woods National Monument*, originally published in 1992 by the Golden Gate National Parks Association, he shared that Mia Monroe—the park ranger we had interviewed earlier that very day—had asked him to. Fifteen years later, he was invited to update the book, as the science and our understanding of these trees continues to evolve over time. He told us, "It was a great pleasure both times, especially the second time, because the trees are so damn fascinating." With a glimmer in his eye, John excitedly described how 66 million years ago, the Chicxulub meteor impact "basically reset the clock on all the evolutionary processes, especially in North America. . . . But somehow, the redwoods got through that. . . . They're essentially the same tree that was here 140 million years ago."

Weeks later John sent us this poem to consider, another reminder that the majestic redwood groves we had just witnessed are only a trace of what these forests were before humans logged them nearly to extinction. We appreciate John's reminder of their resilience against all odds, in the face of a catastrophic meteor and human greed, leaving us with hope that we can help restore these majestic trees that refuse to be destroyed.

The Ancient Ones

GREG SARRIS

Excerpt from *Becoming Story: A Journey Among Seasons, Places, Trees, and Ancestors*

There was a woman who wanted to teach me love medicine. Well, there was a man before her, but she was the first to give me a song and ingredients, the most potent of which, in addition to quail droppings, was the golden red pitch from a redwood tree. The older the tree, the better; the pitch from an old tree is richer, more powerful, principally because, as this woman had told me, it contains a longer memory of the forest.

Descriptions of indigenous people's use of the redwood tree abound. Coast redwoods, the tallest and among the oldest trees on earth, are unique to a relatively narrow stretch of land bordering the coast from what we call today southern Oregon down to the Monterey peninsula. Dozens of indigenous nations inhabited—and still inhabit—the region. Surely these people and their distinct cultures coevolved with the magnificent trees. The Yurok and Wivot of northwestern California split square planks from the trees' durable wood for their houses, and from the same hard wood they crafted seafaring canoes. The deep, swift-moving Klamath River was an important travel route for many of the northwestern California Indian nations, and only canoes dug out from the trunks of heavy redwood ensured safety crossing the river and traveling its great length. My people, the Southern Pomo and Coast Miwok of Sonoma and Marin Counties, removed slabs of bark from the trees and leaned the slabs against a center pole to build conical houses, called *kotchas* by the Coast Miwok. Southern Pomo called the slabs of bark *cashi-da,* house skin. Smaller slabs were used to construct acorn granaries, the hard, impenetrable redwood protecting the acorns from pests and rodents and keeping them free from mildew. The hollow of a redwood trunk could also be used to store acorns, as long as the damp ground was covered by rocks and a layer of bay laurel leaves. Young children were known to make dolls from the hairy bark. In his *Ethnographic Notes on the Southwestern Pomo* (1967), ethnographer James Gifford noted even more uses: "The new foliage, warmed in the fire, was applied as a poultice for earache. The gummy sap which accumulated at the bottom of a hollow redwood was also taken as medicine for a run-down condition. It was soaked in water and the liquid was drunk as a tonic."

Nowhere in any of the literature I've read, however, is there mention of the sap used for love medicine. "You mustn't tell anyone we are talking about this," the woman said to me, I felt as much to warn me as to see if I could be trusted.

I was an adult, in my forties, and I knew better. I shouldn't have let myself get into this position with her in the first place. Worse, when she had broached the subject, I'd encouraged her: I listened.

"Listen," she began. 'When I was a young woman, my husband left me for another woman—a girl up north who was much prettier than me. And he was unkind about it. He told me, 'You, girl, aren't pretty. I will get tired of you. Her, I'll never be able to get enough of.' Shortly thereafter, my old aunt, who knew what had happened, approached me. 'You want him back?' she asked. She already knew my answer—and I already knew what she could teach me. It was raining hard, I remember. She looked out the window at the rain—we were living on the old reservation—and she said, 'In four days there will be sun. Then we will go to the redwoods. We will go to the redwoods first where it is dark at noon." . . .

• ✦ •

The natives in the coastal regions of central California—I'm thinking principally of my people, the Southern Pomo and Coast Miwok—seldom ventured far into the redwood forests. For a host of reasons, we regarded the tall trees with great respect, even fear. The forests were so dense, the trees so tall, that before long you could find yourself in total darkness. Amidst countless and similar-looking trunks, you might quickly become lost, unable to see a way out. The dark forests were home to grizzly bears, the most powerful creatures of the land and, at that time, more numerous than people. Other animals knew as much and stayed away. Settlers discovered that they could rush elk and pronghorn to the line of a redwood forest for easy slaughter because the animals would not go into the trees. The Southern Pomo word for a redwood tree is *qasil.* For the forest, often a simple noun is used: *du-weli*, meaning night.

The landscape was our sacred text, and we listened to what it told us. Everywhere you looked there were stories. An outcropping of rocks was what had become of a greedy man's cache of elk meat. Two disrespected women turned themselves into canyon walls impossible to climb. Everything, even a mere pebble, was thought to have power—power an individual could not utilize unless he or she had a special relationship with the pebble. Violation of any aspect of the natural world—people included—would be punished, in some cases even by death. Physical violence was considered the lowest form of warfare; if you struck a person, you only demonstrated to others you had no spiritual power. Cutting down a tree was also considered a violent act. Early ethnographers characterized our culture as being predicated on black magic and fear; but might we not see it for what it was: predicated on profound respect and a fundamental belief that no one of us is the center of the universe? Doesn't this humility help explain how so many people living so close together and speaking so many different languages maintained for so long their sustainable relationships with both one another and the land?

When white people came to the area, we saw how much their values differed from ours. The Kashaya Pomo word for white people is *pala-cha,* or miracles, and an elder told me the reason: When white people entered this land, they killed humans, they killed animals, and they chopped down trees, but instead of getting punished, instead of this violence turning back on them, more white people arrived and the violence continued. We thought they were miraculous. Those ancestors who first encountered Europeans, if only they could see the world today. Not so miraculous after all. The same elder had prophesied that one day white people would come to us to "learn our ways in order to save the earth and all living things. They will want to know [because] they will want to help. I think that day is here. You young people must not forget the things us old ones is telling you."

• ✦ •

When we went into the redwoods, we did so with purpose. We gathered huckleberries and ferns from clearings inside the forest; mushrooms and clover too. We snared rabbits in nets beneath huckleberry bramble. Known routes through the trees connected inland valleys and plains to the ocean, and we used them with caution. Certain people had greater knowledge of the redwoods than others and therefore took more liberties. Human Bears, for instance—individuals who, having been carefully selected and secretly trained by elder cult members, donned grizzly bear hides and were endowed with the strength of the bear—traveled great distances at night through the trees, but even they were careful. There was much to be wary of. There was a tribe of Little People in the forest, humans only two feet tall, rarely amicable, easily irritated. Slug Woman lived in the forest too. At night, near the edge of the woods, you might hear the tinkling of abalone pendants attached to the empty baby cradle she carries or, worse, you might catch sight of the glistening shells. Don't follow, lest she lead you into the trees, only to return you with no memory.

The Little People and Slug Woman have been in the redwood forests a long time. Coyote planted them there when he created the world from the top of Sonoma Mountain with the assistance of his nephew Chicken Hawk. At that time, all of the animals and birds and plants and trees were people. Redwood trees were old people in Coyote's village. They were wise because they were the oldest. It is said that when they took the form of trees, they made themselves the color of blood because they wanted to remind us that we are all the same, that we were all people once from the same village on Sonoma Mountain. They went west and grew tall so we could see them and their red color and remember the story.

• ✦ •

Growing up, I never thought much about redwood trees. They were there, like oak trees, like Santa Rosa Creek, like cars, like Jersey and Holstein cows in the fields outside of town. I worked on dairies as a small kid, and once, searching for a lost heifer—I must've been six or seven—I wandered into a grove of redwoods.

Looking back, I know that the trees must've been relatively young, but I remember now how quickly the forest became dark, and then how I found the heifer, with buzzards perched on her bloated body and stiff legs, halted in their feeding to look at me. . . .

• ✦ •

Later that afternoon, [I] drove to Wohler Bridge on the Russian River. Across the bridge, on the north side of the water, is a stand of redwoods, certainly not first- or second-growth trees, but tall enough. These were the trees that had come to mind when the woman mentioned redwoods and the Russian River. The water was clear and shallow enough for a person to wade to the trees on the other side. The trees looked dark, a wall of trunks and thick foliage on the riverbanks. The temperature inside the stand felt cool, even cold at times, no matter how warm the summer day. Once, a friend, barefoot and naked in the trees, undoubtedly either not knowing or not thinking about my heritage, said, "Wow! This must've been what it was like being an Indian around here." I might've laughed and asked for whatever it was he was smoking. I didn't tell him what crossed my mind, what I thought about the place just a stone's throw from the beach, where the old folks gathered herbs for colds and asthma. Or how half a mile north of the beach a jealous man murdered my grandmother's aunt and left her under a thicket of willow. Or how first-generation Filipino men fought roosters under the bridge.

Much has changed here. The river is deep and still in the summer. The water, a putrid green, is unhealthy. "No Trespassing" signs line property on both banks. But the trees are still there. The county maintains a small regional park and has placed picnic tables under the redwoods and provided a lot where seasonal visitors pay a fee for parking. Seated at a table, I let my mind wander. Had

I always been able to hear cars passing over the bridge? I couldn't remember being able to see the river from inside the trees, like I could now. What had changed? Was it the park visitors—now a couple walking their dog—that distracted me?

Memories appeared and fled. I thought of looking for pitch, maybe on one of the tree trunks or perhaps oozing from a broken branch, the woman hadn't said where to look. Her babbling about love medicine felt remote now. Why had I taken time to come here? Any sense of urgency that I'd felt hearing her talk, and even the sense of urgency and awe these trees might inspire, escaped me. This grove couldn't have been where she'd come with her aunt to learn about love medicine.

I walked to the road and onto the bridge, where I could look down on the dirty water. I remembered the warm sand, the shallow, clear river. Talk of redwood trees and the river reminded me of those carefree days. I watched a pair of sparrows dart back and forth above the water. I didn't see an osprey, but maybe I just hadn't waited long enough. . . .

• ✦ •

The oldest redwood trees in Sonoma County live in Armstrong Redwoods State Reserve. One tree is fourteen hundred years old, another 310 feet high. Today the eight-hundred-acre reserve features picnic facilities, an outdoor amphitheater, and self-guided nature trails, but the main attraction is the ancient redwood grove, which the parks webpage notes is "a living reminder of the magnificent primeval redwood forest that covered much of this area before logging operations began during the nineteenth century." According to the website, "Colonel James Armstrong, an early-day lumberman, recognized the beauty and natural value of the forests he harvested [and] set aside the area as a 'natural park and botanical garden." But of course he hadn't "discovered" this natural wonder; local natives had lived beside it for centuries. Why hadn't I thought of *these* trees when I was told about love medicine?

[I] drove to Armstrong State Reserve, just outside of Guerneville, on the Russian River. More and more, I'd been thinking about love medicine, of the woman's mention of pitch from old trees. I wasn't interested in collecting the sap, or even seeing it—that is, if I was even able to find it. And anyway, I never did hear about the other necessary ingredients for the love medicine, and I'd long ago heeded Mabel McKay's advice to go about romance "the regular way." . . .

• ✦ •

It was late afternoon when I arrived, the autumn sun already low in the sky, the day still unseasonably warm. From the parking lot, the trees were magnificent indeed, towering above the blacktop and cars. Each trunk was the size of a dozen people huddled together. Wisps of poison ivy lined a path to the picnic tables, the autumn-red leaves like lights announcing the forest.

Inside the forest, seated at a picnic table, I watched as the narrow columns of light filtering through the trees changed color, orange to red-violet. I thought of the things I knew. Was I seeing in that interplay of light and forest a thread for my imagination? The darkening light had to be the color of redwood pitch. Here, in these trees, the last Pomo woman who knew the ingredients and song for love medicine had walked with her old aunt for the first time. Kiss my ass. Isn't that what she'd said to the husband who'd jilted her? When the whale was at the mouth of the Gualala River, did water cover the forest here? The sharp scent of redwoods, pungent in the warm air, reminded me of sand beside a clean river. As daylight waned, the trees seemed to grow taller. I wanted to feel myself grow even smaller beneath them. But that didn't happen. I contented myself with what I'd seen earlier in that interplay of light and forest, that long play of history, the interrelatedness of all things, what I had understood in a single color—the color of pitch from a redwood tree. I saw my place in that history. And there was one thing more.

Days later the weather changed. Fog returned. My house sits high enough on Sonoma Mountain so that, looking west from my kitchen window, I can see the fog covering the Santa Rosa plain to form an inland sea. On that morning, I could see the tops of the trees on the coastal hills poking above the fog. That is how the trees must've looked as my ancestors watched the ocean recede. And then the woman was there, above the fog and smiling confidently, just as she had when she'd said goodbye to me from her front door, only now she was saying hello. I understood. She never taught me love medicine. Maybe never cared to. What she did do for me was enough. The trees. I couldn't forget.

About This Story

Greg Sarris is the tribal chairman of Graton Ranchería, a federally recognized tribe of Coast Miwok and Southern Pomo groups who span Marin and Sonoma Counties along the southern end of the Redwood Coast region. In addition to this role, he's president of the tribe's economic development board, which oversees the tribe's business interests including its resort and casino. He's also an accomplished author with several published novels, including *Grand Avenue*, a collection of short stories adapted into a HBO miniseries that Sarris co-produced with Robert Redford. This story is included in his first collection of essays, focused on his own life, and delves into the meaning of having a deep connection to the place where you live—particularly a place where your ancestors lived and walked since time immemorial.

One thing we were warned of early in our travels was misconceptions of Indigenous people and their relationship to the redwood forests. Whether in regard to inhabiting the forests, utilizing the forests and their resources, or forest management, often the Indigenous perspective is wildly misunderstood. Aside from recent changes to place names and land acknowledgment signage, we felt an absence of the Indigenous viewpoint along the trails and in the parks during our visit and found that many nonnative locals were unfamiliar with the relationship between Indigenous people and redwood forests. We appreciate that Greg's essay highlights the trees' cultural and spiritual significance, and shares how and why Coast Miwok and Southern Pomo people used sophisticated land management techniques like controlled burns.

What We Save

JERRY MARTIEN

Headwaters Forest Reserve

Unrooted, unsteady biped, except for a few surviving maples—maybe a spruce, perhaps a yew—I'm the oldest living thing in these woods.

Huge redwood stumps beside the trail mark the beginning of the end. They took everything they could, then came back for more.

Farther upriver, over the ridge, the grove of old growth the tourists come to see. Call ahead for an appointment.

At the first opportunity I leave the paved path, follow a dirt trail into a grove of young redwood and spruce. This used to be the backyard of Pacific Lumber's caretaker and his wife. Their little house was long ago torn down, for the same reason they were put here—to keep those 1960s people from moving into the abandoned company town. The company forest.

The trail winds through an understory of mostly fern, following a bend in the river. I always stop at the overlook, see how high and muddy the water is in winter, how low and choked by weeds in summer. When it's running clear it reminds me of a stream I fished when I was a kid in southern California.

Then I walk on, thinking about the forest.

On the litter of
needles and
squirrel-gnawed
spruce cones
part way across the trail
a male I guess by his size
(about 5 inches nose to tail)
not moving
a smear of mud on his back

a newt.

In this valley of coastal redwood, these mixed and mismanaged trees have an outside chance of becoming a forest again, given a few centuries and favorable conditions.

Redwoods evolved for longevity, made their bark and wood an irritant to whatever might want to cut or mill or eat them. Should their tiny seeds fail to root, they sprout another tree from twisty knots of burl. The burl is backed up by another system—part tree root, part mycelial earth—by which living trees can send up sprouts from fallen trees or old stumps.

Yet none of that could save them from steel saws and axes.

The newt is another piece of this survival network, too small and slow for our notice. The kind of thing that gets stepped on.

I sit on my heels.
Extend my hand.
With two fingers
I stroke the dried mud
on the rough skin of his back.

Did a hiking boot
tromp you?

He doesn't move.

The newt is a member of the salamander family. Blunt-nosed, lizardlike creatures, the Salamandridae are a keystone species in most of the earth's woodlands. Distinguished by an ability to regenerate lost organs and limbs, they devour worms, slugs, and insects that would otherwise consume trees as insatiably as humans.

Orange-bellied or California newts (*Taricha torosa*) are most prevalent in the state's northern coastal forests. Small and apparently defenseless, *Taricha* turns out to be the most powerful of the redwood's toxic defenses. His pores secrete tetrodotoxin, a powerful and deadly poison.

Like an ancient
reptilian
tai chi master
he raises
his left
foreleg
toes extended.

Newts begin life as aquatic larvae. Known as efts in their terrestrial juvenile phase, they continue to absorb moisture through their permeable skin and in adulthood return to streams or ponds to mate and deposit their eggs. Besides forest, newts require clean water.

Taricha torosa is a California Species of Special Concern, threatened especially in its southern range by invasive species and human habitation.

Leg
lifted

he turns
slowly
to his

left.

Do you
want to cross the
trail?

Logging the old-growth forest inflicted a wound barely beginning to heal when Pacific Lumber was swallowed up by a Texas junk bond artist in 1987. For two decades he made his balloon payments with old-growth redwood, till landslides, floods, and public demonstrations forced the government to step in.

In small watersheds like this, the effect was comparable to scraping off mountaintops to get coal out from under them. Floodwaters and several feet of mud inundated homes, gardens, and orchards, and all but ended the runs of salmon that for ages had come upriver to spawn and leave their bodies to nourish the forest.

With four
fingertips
of each hand
under his orange belly
I lift him.

One ancient grove, plus this second-growth remnant—less than 7,500 acres total—was set aside. Pacific Lumber's mills and inventory and nearly 200,000 acres went to its present owner, who also owns the Oakland A's, now moving to Las Vegas.

Upstream from here, and throughout his holdings, he's moving redwoods to a lumber yard near you.

Like the newt, the systems that are its best means of recovery have not been protected.

He spreads
the four
toes
of each
foot.

Flying newt pose.

Like most of our parks and reserves, this remnant was spared because people put their bodies in the way. And like here, timber companies have cut the best and received millions in taxes and donations for remnants that were said to be saved.

In every way they can find or invent, watershed councils, salmon groups, activist lawyers struggle to make that true. To make it too expensive—too toxic—to take it all. But they, too, get stepped on.

Across
the trail
I set him down
under a maidenhair fern.

Despite how long it takes, how often they lose in courtrooms or get dragged out of the woods in handcuffs, they go on with the work.

Organizing. Meeting. Digging. Meeting some more. Taking out dikes and dams. Planting trees. Hoping to outlive a culture that leaves its muddy bootprint on everything in its way.

All four
feet
on the
tree-
rooted
earth.

It was recovery and repair that brought many people here more than half a century ago. A lot of them were veterans of wars, both at home and abroad. The healing began with themselves, and they applied its lessons to this damaged land.

Natural resource schools taught the science. Tree-planting collectives and watershed groups gave us innovative social structures. Tribes and Indigenous knowledge reminded us that it takes more than technical solutions. Fixing the earth is a way of life.

Instead of lumber, those lessons may come to be our most vital export. This damaged earth knows how to save itself—but if we don't figure out how to work with that knowledge, the earth may well go on without us. It's a lesson that's forgotten but will soon be much in demand.

He's
not
moving.

Did I save the newt? I'll never know. I realize later I moved him away from the river—what if he was going the other direction? Did I interrupt a river rendezvous?

Saving even one small newt is beyond me. Save a forest? We do what we can.

Taricha torosa will be our totem: one foot raised, turning left, a movement too slow to see or understand.

I return
to the paved trail.

As long as I
live
as slowly
as I can
I'll be walking here.

About This Story

Jerry Martien, author and poet, began writing about forests in the 1970s when "a hermitage in the redwoods was interrupted by a nearby clear-cut." In 1990, he was living on the outskirts of Humboldt Bay, working to protect dunes and coastal forest from off-road vehicles during what was known as Redwood Summer, a series of direct actions and protests that were part of a broader environmental campaign to protect the remaining old-growth redwood forests from logging. When he and his wife moved to a house along the Elk River at Headwaters Forest just as the Maxxam Corporation was liquidating the last groves of old-growth coastal redwoods, he was motivated by the log trucks traveling by their house six days a week, beginning at dawn, to dedicate his time to writing for the trees.

Martien, we soon learned, is a man playful with words and enamored by burls. Writing of them, he says, "A burl is a clock. An organism telling time. Through a thousand years and the waves of destruction, a message whispered from the forest beneath the forest." We stumbled upon his books of poetry at Northtown Books in Arcata, where we learned he's a mentor, teacher, and an active part of the Redwood Coast writing community. When we reached out to see if he'd be interested in submitting work for the book, his response included a note that he'd be "attaching a small truckload of redwood stuff" including "a few burls," an affectionate way he refers to his essays. We appreciate his ability to draw us in closer to the often-overlooked tiny friends of a redwood forest when our heads are busy craning up, and to slow us down to newt speed, as he describes it, in his use of line breaks and poetry throughout this piece. He also connected us with a few writers he referred to as "younger and smarter" than him, including contributor Annette Boushey Holland.

The Woman Who Saved Founders Grove

ANNETTE BOUSHEY HOLLAND

When Laura Perrott Mahan and her husband, James, arrived in Dyerville Flats the morning of November 24, 1923, loggers from Pacific Lumber Company were cutting the old-growth redwood trees. Pacific Lumber owned the grove, but they had promised not to log until the conservation community had had time to raise funds to buy it.

Laura and James jumped out of their car and rushed toward the sound of chopping axes and the whine of a new diesel-powered saw the company had just started using to buck up fallen giants. At least twenty huge trees lay on the ground. Fallers were about to drop another one.

The couple confronted the foreman, but he said he had his orders. When she realized there was no way to convince him to stop the logging, Laura stepped into the line of fall of the tree the men were cutting into and faced them.

The men yelled at her to get out of the way—that she was risking her life. But Laura would not back down.

Nearly one hundred years later, in May 2024, my husband and I arrive at the grove, now part of Humboldt Redwoods State Park. We step out of our car into a parking lot with around a dozen cars. We're surrounded—as Laura and James were in their day—by some of the tallest redwoods left on earth. And despite the parking lot and nearby restrooms—one with its door open, a banner of toilet paper waving in the breeze—a sense of awe comes over us.

I'm certainly glad that the park, with help from Save the Redwoods League, plans to relocate the restrooms and parking lot away from the grove and to restore the forest floor. A few years from now, visitors will leave their cars in a former railroad yard and follow an accessible trail into the serenity of the ancient trees.

All around us in the forest, at the base of massive redwoods that reach up into unknown worlds, ancestor trees lie on the ground. Logs that have started to decay spring back into life as nurse logs, supporting gardens of ferns, huckleberries, starflowers, tanoak, and eager young redwoods.

New trees from old logs
Sequoia sempervirens
Everlasting life

A year and a half before Laura's confrontation with the loggers, another historic event occurred in this grove. The California Federation of Women's Clubs was holding its annual convention in Eureka, the first time the small logging town had hosted such a large gathering. Laura had issued the invitation as part of her effort to build support for the redwoods by bringing people to see them.

For years Laura and her friends had watched massive clear-cuts spread around their town and throughout the county, taking more and more of the irreplaceable forest. They said, over and over: "We need to save at least some of the trees for our children's children."

They had lobbied public officials at the county, state, and national levels. Laura had led many tours of the forest. She'd persuaded the Federation to lobby for state funding to purchase redwoods along the new highway in Humboldt County.

The Eureka Inn was newly open for business. A railroad line from San Francisco had just been completed. Now was the chance to bring the women to the trees.

On the last day of the convention—which brought in one thousand delegates—the women, in their long dresses and bonnets, boarded a train for a tour. They passed by lumber mills and denuded mountainsides before arriving in this grove, where their lunch was served on tables covered with white linen and adorned with flowers.

As the keynote speaker, Laura urged the women to help protect the magnificent trees by acquiring the grove for a park. She told them of the company's promise to hold off on logging, and they all donated money. They also promised to write letters, circulate petitions, and lobby their representatives. The movement to create a redwood park was gaining momentum.

One of the delegates recollected later in the *Los Angeles Times* how club members had traveled from all over the state. "A thousand of them gathered in the forest, and there among the trees, whose boles the sunlight had not touched for a thousand years, in the dim forest at noonday, they clasped their hands and pledged themselves to Conservation—the Hope of Civilization."

Beneath the tall trees
I've come to join hands with you,
Long ago sisters

Greg and I cross the parking lot to a sidewalk with several interpretive signs. These signs are new, replacing old ones that told, exclusively, the story of the three men who started Save the Redwoods League in 1918—the founders this grove memorializes—but left out the local women. A new photo depicts early leaders of the league—ten elderly white men—at a dedication ceremony.

It was actually Laura Perrott Mahan who first invited the men from Save the Redwoods League to come north to see the really big redwoods and to hear how the local women were trying to protect them. Both contingents must have been impressed with what the other could offer, because they worked together from then on. The women didn't join Save the Redwoods League, however. Instead, perhaps wanting to maintain their independence, they founded the Humboldt County Women's Save the Redwoods League and elected Laura to serve as president.

One of the new signs tells us that the Lolangkok people have "lived respectfully among and cared for these redwoods" since time immemorial, and that the arrival of European immigrants led to genocide of tribal members. Another pays tribute to the California Federation of Women's Clubs. We even find a picture of Laura Perrott Mahan and the plaque dedicated to her and her husband, hidden in the underbrush for many years but now accessed by a well-marked trail.

We finally step off the asphalt onto a wide trail leading straight to Founders Tree, the biggest of any around. A wooden platform at the base offers a place to pose for photographs without disturbing roots. Low wooden fences around the periphery separate the trail from sections of forest where trampled vegetation needs protection to recover.

Behind the fences, the forest floor fills in with sword ferns, a carpet of oxalis with pale pink flowers, trilliums that have bloomed and dropped their petals, salal, a few tanoaks, and sprigs of poison oak.

As we walk, the trail narrows. I take in the fragrance of the forest, aware of the soft drone of cars on the nearby freeway. The whine of a motorcycle on the Avenue of the Giants intensifies, then subsides. Sunlight infuses the green foliage overhead with a golden glow. Birds sing around us.

Wind in high branches
We fall silent and listen—
Timeless, sacred realm

Greg and I walk past a snag, its jagged top a sculpture with gaps like windows opening to an inside hollow—a room with charred black walls. We see from the bare, trampled ground that this spacious snag is a popular playhouse. Founders Grove, like most of the redwood parks, seems to attract more visitors now than ever before.

It's a trend that Laura foresaw, predicting that someday, if enough of them were protected, the ancient trees would draw visitors to the county and would become an economic mainstay. But not everyone shared her vision, and after Laura and her friends were unable to accomplish their goal through persuasion, she was forced to take her stand.

There are differing versions of what happened when Laura confronted the loggers. The evening of November 23, Laura and James had heard that Pacific Lumber was secretly cutting trees in Dyerville Flats. Before daybreak the couple headed south—a four-hour drive—on the winding roads.

Some people say that Laura climbed on top of a stump, others that she more likely waded into the bed of branches loggers made to cushion a falling tree. However she did it, Laura's action—and the resulting publicity—had a huge impact.

Headlines appeared in the local paper the following morning—November 25—so Laura and James must have made it back to Eureka in time to alert friends who owned the *Humboldt Times*. Or else Laura sent James to get a restraining order and notify the papers while she stayed and held off the loggers.

News of the secret logging outraged the community. The board of supervisors called an emergency meeting that afternoon. Laura's women's club friends, along with a wide range of supporters, packed the courthouse. The next day, the supervisors voted to obtain an injunction and proceed with the acquisition of 160 acres of North Dyerville Flat.

Pacific Lumber Company defiantly countered with its own lawsuit, refusing to sell and saying that the county had no right to condemn its land. The lawsuit halted the county's condemnation plans, but the public support garnered by Laura and the Humboldt County women proved to be crucial. The eventual outcome—Save the Redwood League's purchase of Dyerville Flats and nearby Bull Creek Flats—would not have been possible if Laura Perrott Mahan and her friends hadn't stopped the logging.

Ahead of her time
Or in tune with the timeless
She stood for the trees

Greg and I arrive at the Mahan plaque, attached to a rock beside a low stump left behind after the lumber company's aborted logging operation. On the plaque we see bronze busts of James and—set behind him and looking over his shoulder—of Laura. Even though Laura devoted herself for decades to protecting the redwoods and James played a supporting role, his image is out in front.

Unfortunately, the failure to give credit to the women continues. According to the staff of Humboldt Redwoods State Park, 35 percent of the old-growth redwood we have today was protected by women. At least groves like the Women's Federation Grove and the Garden Club of America Grove were named in their honor. And the wonderful book *Who Saved the Redwoods?* has shed light on the role of women.

On our walk back, we pass a huge fallen log called the Dyerville Giant. Walking beside this mammoth tree is a humbling experience. Lying on its side, the Giant looms twice as high as Greg is tall. And it's a trek of 362 feet from the massive root wad to the other end. The Giant was brought down by wind during a fierce storm in 1991. The tall trees, especially on forest edges, are vulnerable to wind. I worry that as climate change–fueled storms grow more intense, the blowdown will be worse.

Laura and her friends said frequently that they were saving the big redwoods for future generations. The job is clearly not done. The old-growth redwoods, even in parks, aren't safe—threatened not only by increasingly fierce storms but also by mega-fires, floods, and droughts brought on by the climate crisis.

Laura Perrott Mahan and other members of the Humboldt County Women's Save the Redwoods League dedicated much of their lives to conserving the natural world. They weren't well connected like the men who founded Save the Redwoods League. But they were connected with the redwoods, especially in Dyerville Flats, with future generations of children, and with their hearts.

Today, thinking about our grandchildren's futures, we have not only trees to consider but also the entire community of life. We have what seems like an overwhelming amount to do, to protect the earth's intricate life support systems. Saving trees is at least a way to start, and they are an ally. As we save them, they may also save us.

About This Story

We were first introduced to Annette Holland by contributor Jerry Martien, who got to know her when she attended his writing workshop and worked on stories about Laura Perrott Mahan for younger readers. When we reached out to see if she might be interested in developing a piece for adults, she responded with enthusiasm. She told us, "Laura not only spent decades working to protect the ancient trees of what is now Founders Grove, she also quite possibly risked her life." She also shared, "My lifelong passion for nature is equaled by my love of stories. I find stories about people who have made sacrifices to protect the natural world to be both fascinating and inspiring."

Retired park ranger Dan Sealy had told us about another woman we can thank for the preservation of the redwoods: Lucille Vinyard, who helped found Citizens for Redwood National Park in 1965 and is considered by many "the mother of Redwood National Park." As we strolled Founders Grove, freshly aware of the hard work of women who saved the redwoods, it was both comical and disheartening to see how their important history was hardly acknowledged, while the accomplishments of men were widely celebrated.

We are thrilled we were able to commission a piece from Annette Holland that would take us through the grove and tell the important story of Laura Perrott Mahan as the park revisits its interpretative information for visitors.

The Legacy of Luna

JULIA BUTTERFLY HILL

Excerpt from *The Legacy of Luna*

Fierce winds ripped huge branches off the thousand-year-old redwood, sending them crashing to the ground two hundred feet below. The upper platform, where I lived, rested in branches about one hundred eighty feet in the air, twenty feet below the very top of the tree, and it was completely exposed to the storm. There was no ridge to shelter it, no trees to protect it. There was nothing.

As the tree branches whipped around, they shredded the tarp that served as my shelter. Sleet and hail sliced through the tattered pieces of what used to be my roof and walls. Every new gust flipped the platform up into the air, threatening to hurl me over the edge.

I was scared. I take that back. I was terrified. As a child, I experienced a tornado. That time I was scared. But that was a walk in the park on a sunny Sunday afternoon compared to this. The awesome power of Mother Nature had reduced me to a groveling half-wit fighting fear with a paper fork.

Rigid with terror, I couldn't imagine how clinging to a tiny wooden platform for dear life could possibly be part of the answer to the prayer I had sent to Creation that day on the Lost Coast. I had asked for guidance on what to do with my life. I had asked for purpose. I had asked to be of service. But I certainly never figured that the revelation I sought would involve taking up residence in a tree that was being torn apart by nature's fury.

Strangely enough, though, that's how it turned out. As I write this at the age of twenty-five, I've been living for more than two years in a two-hundred-foot-tall ancient redwood located on Pacific Lumber property. I have survived storms, harassment, loneliness, and doubt. I have seen the magnificence and the devastation of a forest older than almost any on Earth. I live in a tree called Luna. I am trying to save her life.

Believe me, this is not what I intended to do with my own. . . .

• ✦ •

My next-door neighbors, Jori and Jason, whom I had known for years, along with a friend of theirs named Barry, announced that they were setting out on a trip to the West Coast.

"Our fourth backed out, and we really need someone else to help pay for gas," they told me. "You want to go with us?"

I couldn't have been happier. It wasn't the world, but it was a start. We set off in June. Our group was eager to see Washington's Olympic rain forests, but our travel plans were loose. We met a stranger in passing who told us that if we were heading west, we had to stop in Humboldt County and see the Lost Coast and the redwoods, one of the largest undeveloped coastlines left in this country. I was convinced. We changed course and followed his advice.

After stopping at the magnificent shore, we entered Grizzly Creek State Park to see the California redwood giants. When Jason and Jori learned that their dogs would not be allowed on the trail, they decided to walk the road that circles the campground and admire the redwoods from there.

That wasn't enough for me.

"There's something about these trees," I said. "I have to get away from all the tourists and the cars and really get out in this forest."

"Well, Julia, we're only gonna stay for a few minutes, maybe fifteen minutes tops," they countered.

"No problem," I answered. "If I'm not back when you're ready to go, just leave my stuff at the ranger's station and tell them I'll be glad to pay however much it costs to store it there. But I'm going out."

As I crossed the highway, I felt something calling to me. Upon entering the forest, I started walking faster and faster, and then, feeling this exhilarating energy, I broke into a run, leaping over logs as I plunged in deeper.

After about a half mile, the beauty of my surroundings started to hit me. I slowed down for a better look. The farther I walked, the larger the ferns grew, until they were so big that three people with outstretched arms couldn't have encircled them. Lichen, moss, and fungus sprouted everywhere. Around each bend in the path, mushrooms of every shape and size imaginable burst forth in vivid hues of the rainbow. The trees, too, became bigger and bigger. At first they seemed like normal trees, but as I leaned my head back as far as I could, I looked far up into the air. I couldn't even see their crowns. Hundreds of feet high, they were taller than fifteen-, eighteen-, even twenty-story buildings. Their trunks were so large that ten individuals holding hands would barely wrap around them. Some of the trees were hollow, scorched away by lightning strikes, yet they still stood. These trees' ancestors witnessed the dinosaur days. Wrapped in the fog and the moisture they need to grow, these ancient giants stood primordial, eternal. My feet sank into rich earth with each step. I knew I was walking on years upon years of compounded history.

As I headed farther into the forest, I could no longer hear the sounds of cars or smell their fumes. I breathed in the pure, wonderful air. It tasted sweet on my tongue. Everywhere I turned, there was life whether I could see, smell, hear, taste, or touch it or not. For the first time, I really felt what it was like to be alive, to feel the connection of all life and its inherent truth—not the truth that is taught to us by so-called scientists or politicians or other human beings, but the truth that exists within Creation.

The energy hit me in a wave. Gripped by the spirit of the forest, I dropped to my knees and began to sob. I sank my fingers into the layer of duff, which smelled so sweet and so rich and so full of layers of life, then lay my face down and breathed it in. Surrounded by these huge, ancient giants, I felt the film covering my senses from the imbalance of our fast-paced, technologically dependent society melt away. I could feel my whole being bursting forth into new life in this majestic cathedral. I sat and cried for a long time. Finally, the tears turned into joy and the joy turned to mirth, and I sat and laughed at the beauty of it all. . . .

Tree-sitting is a last resort. When you see someone in a tree trying to protect it, you know that every level of our society has failed. The consumers have failed, the companies have failed, and the government has failed. Friends of the forests have gone to the courts, activists have tried to make consumers aware, but with no results. Corporations have neglected their responsibility as landowners, while the government has refused to enforce its laws. Everything has failed, so people go into the trees.

"I have no other way to stop what's happening" is basically what a tree-sitter is saying. "I have no other way to make people aware of what's at stake. I've followed the rules, but everything I've been told to do is failing. So it's my responsibility to give this one last shot, to put my body where my beliefs are."

Efforts to preserve the coast redwoods date back to the early 1900s, when four society women from Eureka, California, birthed the movement by forming the Save-the-Redwoods League. Dressed in fur-trimmed coats and fancy hats, they wrote letters to politicians as well as to a number of renowned and moneyed naturalists. Then they took their cause on the road, just as today's protesters have taken their cause to the trees, in order to promote public awareness. Without these past and present activists, more of California's ancient forests would have fallen long ago.

Though Luna started as an Earth First! tree-sit, I wasn't—and still am not—part of that group. In truth, I didn't even know what Earth First! was until my second stint in the tree. All I wanted to do was have a purpose and direction in my life. Helping save the ancient forest seemed like the urgent answer to a question I didn't even know I was asking. I really didn't care what group sponsored which actions.

From the very start, sitting in Luna gave me a sense of purpose. Here was something I could do to make a difference. Of course, I had no idea that this would mean abandoning the ground for two years. And I had no idea what the forces of nature—and a company called Pacific Lumber/Maxxam—would soon unleash upon my head. . . .

• ✦ •

The moment the storm hit, I couldn't have climbed down if I had wanted to. To climb you have to be able to move, and my hands were frozen. Massive amounts of rain, sleet, and hail mixed together, and the winds blew so hard I might have been ripped off a branch.

The storm was every bit as strong as they said it would be. Actually, up here, it was even stronger. When a gust would come through, it would flip the platform up into the air, bucking me all over the place.

"Boy! Whoaaah! Ooh! Whoa!"

The gust rolled me all the way up to the hammock. Only the rope that cuts an angle underneath it prevented me from slipping through the gap in the platform.

"I'm really ready for this storm to chill out. I'm duly impressed," I decided. "I've bowed and cowered once again before the great almighty gods of wind and rain and storm. I've paid my respects—and my dues—and I'd appreciate it if they got the heck out of here."

My thoughts seemed to anger the storm spirits.

"Whoa! Whoa!" I cried, as the raging wind flung my platform, straining the ropes that attached it.

"This is getting really intense! Oh, my God! Oh, my God! Okay, never mind, I take it back. Whoaaah!"

The biggest gust threw me close to three feet. I grabbed onto the branch of Luna that comes through the middle of the platform, and I prayed.

"I want to be strong for you, Luna. I want to be strong for the forest. I don't want to die, because I want to help make a difference. I want to be strong for the movement, but I can't even be strong for myself."

It seemed like it took all my will to stay alive. I was trying to hold onto life so hard that my teeth were clenched, my jaws were clenched, my muscles were clenched, my fists were clenched, everything in my body was clenched completely and totally tight.

I knew I was going to die.

The wind howled. It sounded like wild banshees, *rrahhh,* while the tarps added to the crazy cacophony of noise, *flap, flap, flap, bap, bap, flap, bap*! Had I remained tensed for the sixteen hours that the storm raged, I would have snapped. Instead, I grabbed onto Luna, hugging the branch that comes up through the platform, and prayed to her.

"I don't know what's happening here. I don't want to go down, because I made a pact with you. But I can't be strong now. I'm frightened out of my mind, Luna, I'm losing it. I'm going crazy!"

Maybe I was, maybe I wasn't, but in that moment I heard the voice of Luna speak to me.

"Julia, think of the trees in the storm."

And as I started to picture the trees in the storm, the answer began to dawn on me.

"The trees in the storm don't try to stand up straight and tall and erect. They allow themselves to bend and be blown with the wind. They understand the power of letting go, continued the voice. "Those trees and those branches that try too hard to stand up strong and straight are the ones that break. Now is not the time for you to be strong, Julia, or you, too, will break. Learn the power of the trees. Let it flow. Let it go. That is the way you are going to make it through this storm. And that is the way to make it through the storms of life."

I suddenly understood. So as I was getting chunked all over by the wind, tossed left and right, I just let it go. I let my muscles go. I let my jaw unlock. I let the wind blow and the craziness flow. I bent and flailed with it, just like the trees, which flail in the wind. I howled. I laughed. I whooped and cried and screamed and raged. I hollered and I jibbered and I jabbered. Whatever came through me, I just let it go.

"When my time comes, I'm going to die grinning," I yelled.

Everything around me was being ripped apart. My sanity felt like it was slipping through my fingers like a runaway rope. And I gave in.

"Fine. Take it. Take my life. Take my sanity. Take it all."

Once the storm ended, I realized that by letting go of all attachments, including my attachment to self, people no longer had any power over me. They could take my life if they felt the need, but I was no longer going to live my life out of fear, the way too many people do, jolted by our disconnected society. I was going to live my life guided from the higher source, the Creation source.

I couldn't have realized any of this without having been broken emotionally and spiritually and mentally and physically. I had to be pummeled by humankind. I had to be pummeled by Mother Nature. I had to be broken until I saw no hope, until I went crazy, until I finally let go. Only then could I be rebuilt; only then could I be filled back up with who I am meant to be. Only then could I become my higher self.

That's the message of the butterfly. I had come through darkness and storms and had been transformed. I was living proof of the power of metamorphosis. . . .

At first, the idea of going to the very top of Luna was terrifying. The wind scared me the most. I always felt like I was off balance, that the wind was trying to rip me off the tree. So I'd wait until it wasn't blowing too hard before seeking out new pathways. At each precarious point, I'd have to overcome a new set of fears. My heart jumping out of my skin, I would gather my courage and trust that my bond with Luna would guide me in how, when, and where to climb.

Eventually I felt comfortable climbing behind the platform, which is not easy. To go above that, however, meant negotiating many branches that, having been exposed to such extreme weather, are thin and brittle. Still, I felt a constant calling to go to the top.

Maybe it was the feeling that drives people to hike mountains, that feeling of making it to the highest place possible, that inner urge to find our higher self. Some people think its about an adrenaline rush or conquering, but I think it's a constant striving we have inside ourselves. I don't like the feeling of conquering. We conquer a mountain because we can climb it, then we conquer a mountain because we can blow it up for tunnels and highways and mineral extraction. We play God and destroy the natural balance.

So for me, climbing to the top was not conquering Luna. I just felt compelled to reach it. Once I learned how to disperse my weight among both hands and feet instead of placing it all on a single branch, I thought, "I can do this!"

So I tried. As I climbed in my bare feet—which I didn't wash so that the sap would help me stick to the limbs—I spoke to Luna. In return, she guided me to those branches that were safe and warned about those that were not. Without shoes, I could feel her underneath me and understand her messages.

I made it to her lightning-hardened pinnacle, the most magical spot I'd ever visited. Luna is the tallest tree on the top of the ridge. Perched above everything and peering down, I felt as if I was standing on nothing at all, even though this massive, solid tree rose underneath me. I held on with my legs and reached my hands into the heavens. My feet could feel the power of the Earth coming through Luna, while my hands felt the power of the sky. It was magical. I felt perfectly balanced. I was one with Creation.

No way could I allow Luna to be cut! Ever! . . .

At last, it was time to go. During one of my last nightly climbs to the top platform to plug in a battery to the charging system, I climbed out onto one of my favorite branches of Luna and nestled in to her loving embrace. It was a gorgeous evening with the fog slowly rolling into the Eel River valley down below and a crystal clear sky above. The waxing moon brightly lit much of the sky and made the fog glow iridescently. A few stars shimmered at the edge of my view. It was a scene I had seen many times over the past two years—each time slightly different, each time breathtaking. As I sat there taking it all in, I realized that this was to be one of the last times I would ever look out at this view that had become as much a part of me as the experience had. I burst into tears.

Later that night I wrote, "I feel like I'm being separated from a part of myself—a piece of me—the essence of who I am. The woman I have become is being torn right now. I am beginning to feel the understanding—the never-ending lesson of letting go. When I leave this tree, I will be leaving the best friend I've ever had. It is a pain I can not describe, only feel... and be with. I am with it now, and it is only the beginning. I will be able to come back and be with Luna in her womb at her base, but never again will I perch in her branches viewing the world from this incredible perspective. I will do my best to live the rest of my life in honor of her and this experience—offering myself as the only gift I have to give. It is my prayer and my hope that I will always and only be an offering."

A few days later, as I prepared to descend Luna for the first time in 738 days, which would also be the last time, I began to sob once again. How would I be able to keep the focus, grounding, and truth that I had found in Luna? How would I be able to keep going when it felt like I was dying, having to leave this incredible living being?

I prayed, and for the last time in her branches, Luna spoke to me and reminded me of something I had received in prayer nearly a year before: "Julia, all you have to do when you are afraid, lonely, worn out, or overwhelmed is touch your heart. Because it is there that I truly am, and it is there I will always be."

About This Story

Julia Butterfly Hill—"Butterfly" being a nickname honoring the time one landed on her when she was a girl and stayed with her throughout the duration of a hike—belongs to a lineage of women who have put their bodies on the line, literally, to save the trees. She is a local legend for her 738-day tree sit, an extraordinary form of direct action during the tense Timber Wars of the 1990s that pitted environmentalists against loggers. We first learned about Hill in the bookstore in Muir Woods when we came across the beautifully illustrated children's book *Luna & Me: The True Story of a Girl Who Lived in a Tree to Save a Forest* by Jenny Sue Kostecki-Shaw. Our interest piqued, we soon found Hill's own *The Legacy of Luna: The Story of a Tree, a Woman, and the Struggle to Save the Redwoods.*

Hill's book details what led her from life as an "average teenager" in Arkansas with "regular dreams of a regular person" to living in a nearly two-thousand-year-old redwood tree at age twenty-five. She suffered a brain injury in a car accident in the mid-1990s, largely impacting the left side of her brain, which, according to Hill, enabled her right, more creative side, to kick in and help shift her perspective and values in life for the better. The book follows her journey after a year of intensive therapy as she explores a life focused on the legacy she will leave behind. She begins with a spontaneous trip to the redwoods in 1997, where she ultimately scales a 1,500-foot redwood tree in Humboldt County named Luna to save it from logging.

Given there are very few people who can say they've lived in the canopy of a redwood tree, we thought these snippets from her autobiography would allow readers to live vicariously through her words without all that climbing. For ourselves, we know we'd rather read about being caught in a storm nearly 200 feet up in a redwood canopy than experience it firsthand.

We Who Hold Up the World

SHAUNNA OTEKA MCCOVEY

When the Spirit Beings came to make the world for humans, they pondered how the people would live. How would they cross rivers, for they had no wood? As they sat near the Klamath and thought about this, someone suddenly sprung up from the earth and grew very fast. The Spirit Beings wanted to know its name, and it answered, "Do you not know who I am? I am called Redwood (Keehl) and they will make boats of me and cross the river. They will put pitch on my head and pitch on my stern and a necklace around my neck. This is the way I like it." The Spirit Beings rejoiced at Redwood's arrival because they knew the humans would now live properly.

—IN YUROK MYTHS

K*eehl* came to us during creation, solidifying the relationship between Yurok people and the redwood as one of reciprocity, respect, and responsibility. *Keehl* is our relative, our protector, our guardian, and as the story above depicts, our interdependent relationship with this Spirit Being who became a tree allows us to truly live properly.

In our culture everything is alive. Everything has an energy and a place and role in our society. *Keehl's* role is significant. Our traditional houses are made of redwood plank, the stools we sit on in our houses are made of redwood, and canoes that allow us to travel the rivers are made of redwood. When the *ohl-we'-yoch* is carved, it is given kidneys, a heart, and lungs. Its heart beats and its lungs breathe in sync as boat and paddler become one on the water. Every ride we take in a canoe reestablishes our connection to the being that gave itself to become a boat so we could survive. Every ride we take, we thank it.

When I was in college at Humboldt State University, I used to pass by one of our traditional canoes every time I went to the library. The canoe sat at the entrance to a stairwell on the first floor. There was a sign placed in front of it that said, "Please do not touch." I always ignored the sign and greeted the boat with words and with touch. I thanked *Keehl* for becoming a boat. I put my hands on its heart so it could feel my presence. I knew it was alive and I knew it must have been lonely there in the stairwell, on display but longing to be on the water. This canoe was also special to me because some years earlier my dad had helped build it. He was a student a few years before me at Humboldt and part of the group of carvers who spent months making the boat. I remember how happy he was to be part of its creation and how excited he was when he shared with me details of the canoe's first journey on Humboldt Bay. My dad put part of himself into the boat, and so I was part of it, too. I tried to make it feel loved whenever I could. It did the same for me during the times I felt lonely and out of place in college. I would often go and visit the canoe so I could feel closer to my dad, closer to home, and closer to Creation.

The redwood log used by my dad and his carving crew was acquired through a grant and originated somewhere in Redwood National and State Parks. If not for the creation of the national park in 1933, there probably wouldn't be any redwoods left on the North Coast. The timber companies were bent on logging every last tree, and we Tribal people were not in any position to defend them.

Though the Parks stepped in at a critical time in history, only 5 percent of old-growth redwoods remain. Ninety-five percent of our old guardians are gone forever. It's hard to comprehend, but then so are a lot of things we have lost. In the early years of establishment, the Parks weren't always friendly to Tribal people, especially those requesting logs for canoes or to gather materials for our baskets. There were times when we weren't friendly, either. But to be honest, it's never been easy for us to ask for or to have to buy back, through grants or other means, those things that have always been integral to our way of life—essential parts of our being.

The Tribal relationship with the Parks has evolved since the early 1990s when my dad worked on the canoe, but I don't know if they will ever truly understand the depth of our connection to *Keehl*. Our worldviews are so different. Our belief system is interwoven with reciprocity, the idea that *Keehl* is here to protect us and to be purposed by us for our survival. The Parks see the redwood groves as needing to be preserved, owned and managed by the government for public enjoyment. Which is, of course, not a bad thing. It's just not the same kind of relationship that we share with *Keehl*. Today, we work hard at finding common ground with the Parks in the middle of our differences. We work hard to help them better understand who we are.

Somewhere just downriver from where Blue Creek flows into the Klamath River was a sacred redwood tree that was said to hold up the world. A few miles upriver from this gigantic tree was a smaller grove of redwoods that were integral to our fish dam ceremony near the old village of Kepel. Those trees were extremely important to our cosmology and ceremonial beliefs. They held great responsibilities and we counted on them to do their part. Each of those trees is gone now. The one who held up the world was swept away in a flood. The small grove so essential to the fish dam ceremony was logged, much to the dismay of Yurok people. We couldn't protect them then, but we honor them now by sharing the responsibility, by living right, by living properly. We honor them because we, too, hold up the world. Our high dances are called world renewal ceremonies. When we dance we hold up the world for everyone, for everything. We hold up the world as we carry the prayers of the people up the mountain trail for the Deerskin Dance. We hold up the world as we stamp out the bad and bring back balance during our Jump Dance. We hold up world and make it new.

My call to my people has always been to remember who we are. To remember our beauty and return to ceremony. To remember our responsibility to take care of this place the Spirit Beings made for us. To remember the gifts they gave and that we are not separate from earth and sky, from river and redwood. To remember . . .

> We are river warriors and land reclaimers,
> ocean stewards and dam breakers,
>
> we are fixing the earth
> through songs and smoke and prayer.
>
> We are canoe carvers and basketmakers,
> flower dancers and Milky Way gazers,

we are the night spirits from across-the-ocean-Land,
the People before the Park.

We have redwood hearts and salmon skin,
flicker-feathered hair and tattooed chins,

we are the blood and bones
of those who came before.

We are Deerskin Dance singers and medicine makers,
acorn pickers and baby rattle shakers,

We are Poh-lik-lah, Pey-cheek-lah, Ner-er-ner
We are Keehl

and we hold up the world.

About This Story

We discovered the poetry of Shaunna Oteka McCovey, who is both Yurok and Karuk and a member of the Yurok Tribe, while browsing in the Cal Poly Humboldt (formerly Humboldt State University) special collections. We later learned that she is a graduate and a distinguished alumna of Humboldt State. When we spotted her work again in *Ka'm-t'em: A Journey Toward Healing*, a book on Indigenous knowledge, we knew we needed to include McCovey in this collection and were excited to invite her to write a new piece for *Campfire Stories*.

McCovey is an enrolled member of the Yurok Tribe and grew up on the Yurok and Hoopa Valley Indian Reservations, as well as in Karuk Country in Northern California. Yurok people have always lived in their ancestral territory and there are now four federally recognized Tribes of Yurok people. The institution of more formal tribal governments has given each Tribe a stronger voice and more self-determined future. Tribal sovereignty is of utmost importance to the Tribes in the Redwood region, and they continue to act in ways to uphold their sovereignty, including the stewardship of lands and waters.

McCovey's piece tells us of the three Rs of Yurok wisdom: reciprocity, respect, and responsibility. Many Indigenous scholars will add a fourth R, relationship, but the lessons are the same—that everything is alive and has an energy and role in society, and must be treated as such. *Keehl* is not just a resource, but our relative, our protector, our guardian. This perspective is in stark contrast to that of the 49ers, the Gold Rush prospectors whose mad dash to get rich resulted in the displacement and murder of Native peoples and devastation of the environment.

The Creation

BENJAMIN GREEN

I looked around in the songless air,
at the night that was more than black.
My heart was quiet, the page was blank.

I could feel the fallen sky
sinking into the dark of the
world, wombwet, newborn, and shining.
Mists rose from ink-stains
lying prone on the water, and stretched lengthwise.
Things were coming down with the shade
but I could not see to guess their excellence.
I told myself, *take care, be careful—*
as insects rose in the dawn stillness,
and shaking leaves reflected on the rolling water.
I saw the light shape itself.
My eyes found a place to rest
on alder limbs as they bleached white,
their leaves full of sun and shadow.
Rays shattered down,
dusty shafts turned toward me.
Thus was the world revealed,
a little at a time.

Light took its shape,
by the green serrated fronds of ferns,
in the sharp spikes of reed,
on the rounded shapes of water polished stone.
Great trunks of redwoods
leaned their mossy runneled bark
and wove lichened goat's beard boughs
over the mirroring water.
I saw this wild braided light
in the dawn's mist and
I knew that it was good.

I felt the earth, hard and solid, beneath my bare feet.
The soil took shape as I walked upon it.
Deep grass bent in the sunlight,
straining up, steadying me where I stood.
My fingers dug for what was under the grass,
in the earth, the dark ground,
heavy with seed.
I sensed living things waiting,
all mingled together,
rooted in rock, sapped and sloping,
hefty and marrow-filled,
with one deep duty—renewal.
I looked earthward
and everything held carefully
to the land,
and I knew that it was good.

And, then, I saw the water walking downhill,
hopping over rocks, leaping,
hissing and spitting, whistling and humming its way home,

carrying leaves clear to the beach
where the ocean, scaled like a fish,
lashed them with a salty surf of waves.
The water took shape,
gathered itself in clear running passages,
shining and pulsing, upwelling,
knitting together the world in new membership,
and I knew that it was good.

Finally, I stood under a canopy of birdsong.
Kingfishers and flickers, wrens and swallows,
hawks and wild ducks and vultures
brought breath out of darkness
into the lightfall,
created song in the face of leaves.
Moles dug through the earth,
honeybees drank at flowers,
dragonflies hovered over the water, hawking mosquitoes,
lightfooted deer slept in the tall grass,
elk and bear and foxes, and the big cats prowled.
There was a rain of leaf fall:
redbud, buckeye, twinberry, wax myrtle—
and the towering silence of the redwoods.
In the water, fish were shaping themselves
and I looked at this, all this, my work done,
and I knew it,
I had seen it all before in my mind
and I knew that I could love even what was not intended.
I knew it was good
for it was a living thing.

Listening to My Grandfather

BENJAMIN GREEN

I remember when there were fish.
Great tribes of salmon—
king, silver, red, pink, chum—
speckled rain-swollen rivers
with colorful eggs.
Steelhead, cutthroat, shad,
met annually like revivalists
under swelling tents of green water.

The flesh of trout blessed me.
I watched as rainbows cleared storms,
heard the splash of brookies in mountain tarns,
saw huge German browns
swallow unsuspecting mice,
smelled the rot of mackinaws
after a winter cold enough
to freeze the deep lakes solid.
I saw a thousand stars shine
on the sleeve of a golden trout.

Nothing I ever witnessed washed off
the sins of the world so well
as the sight of a young boy
releasing a native trout
back into the clear fast-flowing water
of a wild river.

How could I accept silt from logged slopes
drifting downstream,
plastic nets washing ashore
on the beach,
pulp mills that squat on the banks
of delicate rivers and bays, flushing
their poisonous toilets into pristine water?
Reservoirs deaden
behind concrete and earthen empoundments,
and dead fry and smolts collect
on the hot gravel of treeless creeks.

I never thought that men
were stronger than fish.
I never thought those great tribes of salmon
would join the grizzly, the tule elk, the condor,
or that I would visit a zoo
to see the captive breeding of fish.

Already, fish are becoming mythic,
half-spirit, half-lie,
Sometimes, even I doubt their existence.
But I can remember

how their dark-finned solidity
gave motion to the morning
light on a still lake,
and how every night
the earth fell into the black sky,
and how every morning
it came home with the halibut
hiding the moon under its belly,
with the eels resting in the kelp,
with the sculpin extending
its spines in the estuary.
It was watching the shadows of fish
that I saw how to make peace with mine.

I remember when there were fish.

About This Story

Poet Benjamin Green wrote his collection *The Sound of Fish Dreaming* while he lived in Trinidad, California, on the Redwood Coast. These poems from that book read like a beginning and an end—a creation and an extinction. We love how the first poem captures the exuberance of life that can be found here along the streams and coastlines, and under the "towering silence of the redwoods." Then, we're reminded how fragile it all really is—how beloved creatures once so abundant can become just a memory to be shared. Fish populations were drastically impacted by logging in the region due to the erosion and runoff from logging roads that washed excess sediment into the water. This, in addition to the removal of trees in and along the creeks, smothered fish eggs and reduced oxygen in the water where fish release and deposit eggs.

Green is the author of eleven books. Now retired, he resides in Jemez Springs, New Mexico, out of a desire to live someplace where he can "go outside every day," where it doesn't rain from November to May. At the age of sixty-eight, he hopes his new work articulates a mature vision of the world and does so with some integrity.

"I Am a Visitor of the Forest"

CALLIE LARA

Excerpt from *Ka'm-t'em: A Journey Toward Healing*

I am a visitor of the forest. I travel gently into an environment sacred to the dwellers.
The brown and gold bracken crunches underfoot.
Twigs and limbs are tangled like webs before me.
Along the perimeter of the trees bear grass shoots sprout up.
In the distance timber circling open prairies allow the day to cast light on the vegetation spread across the ground.
Above me, the dense canopy vibrates the whispering of the trees from one to another. Down the ravine, I hear the songs of flowing water trickling over the rocks.
Rays of light shoot through the limbs, like spears spotlighting the beauty of the landscape.
I smell the aromas that guide the inhabitants, the burst of a budding orchard, ferns, lichen, bark, and the decomposition of the forest in the cycle of life.
I feel the presence of life all around me.
I hesitate at the sound of a large creature lumbering through the brush or the stealth of a feline moving along the branches.

Small animals scurry along the forest terrain in their social practices.
Woodpeckers fall silent as I pass but then quickly alert the residence of my presence.
All that is the forest gives to the prayers of the world.
I am most humbled by the magnificence of the spirit being, the little people, in the mist.
A labyrinth to another dimension of the world I am forbidden to travel.
At this moment, all that I have described falls to the back of my consciousness.
Easily my spirit transcends and time unifies us.
Although only for a moment, I have participated in a phenomenon of time and share the breath of the forest, I am the captive.
I cry out, "I am a visitor of the forest!"

Songs of "Those Within"

CALLIE LARA

Excerpt from *Ka'm-t'em: A Journey Toward Healing*

Intricately shaped abalone shells adorn the prayer items of the Indigenous people of the Hoopa Valley. Their song vibrates across the river from the dance grounds, creating an energy that speaks to ninasa:n (the world) in prayer. The shells slapping together with the song of a waterfall continues to echo off the mountain while dancers stomp the ground and harmonize with the rhythm of the world in ceremonial songs. Clam shells, bull pine, cedar, and juniper berries rustle against each other, mimicking the wind as it beats against the timber that surround the valley floor. Materials are bound together with the natural fibers that flourish within the historic boundaries of my home. The spirit of wildlife, birds, otter, deer, and spiritual beings of the forest and river contribute to the sacred prayers of an ancient people; all the while the patterns of the universe hover just above. "Shea ninas:an," I am present in this moment, we continue prayer as root is fed into the fire, a beacon between human beings and the dimensions of this world and time.

This is my inspiration. I am a regalia maker. I am a member of a society of individuals dedicated to the preservation of our ceremonies. We understand the formulas of an ancient people. There are many stories to be shared of the purpose that keeps us connected to the world, to our environment, and of the spirit animals that carry our prayers. Our ancestors have guided us in the revitalization and restoration of our traditional way of life. I am among many contributors of regalia, ceremonial prayer items, who have survived the colonization and the attempted annihilation of a people. I am Natinixwe (spirit being on a human journey) from Jimekenehutch, Tsewelnaldin, Medilxwe, and the far-off lands of Oklahoma. My ancestors from these places live through me. Me che nai kiwil dichwin il, those within come out and are born again. Alice Pratt ne:en[1], a ceremonial practitioner, began her prayer in this way, referring to our ancestors, our DNA and our genetic memory. Through this concept, historical accounts, and personal events, I will share my story in hopes to give a glimpse of an ancient people. I will begin with my grandmother, Emma Hitchcock Norton. She was an enrolled Cherokee tribal member and grew up the oldest of five sisters in Tahlequah, Oklahoma. Her grandmother, originally from North Carolina, survived the relocation infamously known as the "Trail of Tears" at twelve years old. My grandmother Emma met my grandfather, Jack (Hupa) at Haskell Indian Boarding School. They became educators and made their way back to Hoopa where they remained. My grandmother Emma didn't like to talk about the historical events of her people, but she did share with me a skill in the intricate ribbon work stitching of her grandmothers. I became very comfortable with needle

1 A word to refer to the deceased

and thread at an early age. This is important to me because it is the only connection I have to my grandmother, Emma's people.

I was born and raised in the Hoopa Valley. I was fortunate to be surrounded in the Hupa culture and traditions. Materials that are abundant to our home were placed in our small hands. We—my sisters Holly, Patti and I—learned to twist and braid in hopes to become seasoned weavers; we peeled and stripped roots and maple bark into fine strands and strung shells and beads into necklaces that reflected the life of the ocean. As children we were told, "let your hands do it." I believed it and let my heart and mind follow.

At eleven years old. I made my first xoji kya, ceremonial dance dress, of the Hupa people. I had a cousin named Joelle, attending Berkeley University at the time, who had access to nicely cut abalone from a button factory. In the 1960s, these unique materials were hard to come by. Joelle brought them to me during her summer break. The 1960s had a renewed confidence and interest in the rebuilding of regalia. The sons and daughters, seeking traditional knowledge, used modern threads and materials that were available. That was my mother's generation. Her parents had survived the boarding school era, where traditional ways of doing things were discouraged. My mother's generation bred a new generation, my generation. Although unpopular, we spoke out, foreign Christian teachings, and protested, and began to reclaim our truths. We rejected the injustice, educational institutionalization that swept across Indian Nations and impacted what had been a traditional way of life for almost one hundred years.

For some, higher education presented itself as a way to "beat institutions at their own game." Education was important in "waking up our people," and continues to be an important tool in the preservation of our way of life. With that said, it is also important to embrace the traditional teachings not taught in a classroom but through our ceremonies, prayers, and elders.

I was guided by my grandma Nancy and Grandpa George, in the concepts of the K'winya'nya:n ma ah'winew (the way Indian people do things) that held our people together. This gave me the confidence to complete my first xoji kya dress. Probably somewhat archaic or clumsy in design, it was completed with the haunches of the deer hide wrapping around the hips, with a two-inch pleat in the fold of the hide. The pleat is not only significant to the structure of the dress, but holds a spiritual significance as well. The shells, beads, fringe, and an apron add to the song of the dress. As a child, I completed the dress over the summer, learning the basics of regalia making. "Always work with your materials in a good-way; never take from the environment more then you need; put your things away while in mourning," were lessons shared by everyone. I learned that your feelings could be passed on to your dress or regalia piece. I gifted this first dress to my Grandma Nancy Nixon. Her contributions to our prayers and people impacted me greatly. It was important to her that we learn as much of our language as we could, participate in ceremony and understand the philosophies of the Hupa people. She loved to tell us stories: lessons of coyote, the little people, big foot or the Kixinai, (the ancient people). These stories were and are timeless in meaning. She performed the duties of the medicine for the Hupa ceremonies, the Brush Dance, Jump Dance and White Deerskin Dance, during the late fifties through the early 1970s.

Fifty years later, I watched the morning sun bounce off the abalone shells of the first dress I had made. My first instinct was to offer to remake the dress; however, this dress represented my beginning and a connection to the voices of my grandmothers, "let your hands do it."

Over the years, I have completed nine ceremonial dresses (taking six months to a year to complete each dress) for daughters and grand-daughters, as well as assisted others in the process. Although I have contributed numerous prayer items to our ceremonies, I have never completed a piece alone. There have always been helpers—whether they were gatherers, weavers, carvers, storytellers, hunters, researchers, or elders—that have worked alongside me, forming and shaping my perception. . . .

• ✦ •

For many years, I have spent my seasons gathering and preparing materials, always with an understanding of the piece or its unique relationship to ceremonial prayers. Through whił dinił ay (my mind stretching out from me), I would visualize a design and begin to create. However, at a certain point the piece takes on its own life or spirit and begins to direct me. It becomes itself. There is resistance in trying to manipulate the outcome. When a piece becomes itself, it is a powerful moment. It is when a dress or regalia piece speaks. This is when a regalia maker becomes humbled. The bond, thoughts, and prayers of the work become stronger. For this reason, I have not been able to make a piece for sale nor monetary gain. How could I sell a prayer? I believe the difference between a regalia maker and a jewelry maker is that a jewelry maker has the freedom to creatively blend materials from all over the world and to express their interpretation of their world. A regalia maker is accountable to the prayer of the k'ixinai, the environment, and the K'iwinya'nya:n. We use materials that are referred to by our people as "blessed materials," chosen by the k'ixinai to represent a spirit to the dance, such as the woodpecker for his relationship to his family; the gentleness of the deer; the tenacity of the porcupine; the environmental consciousness of the humming bird, or the prayer of an abalone. Although binding materials have changed over the years, the blessed spirits have not. . . .

• ✦ •

Hai me:w nas:sita:n, the ceremonial Jump Dance headdress, reflects the layers of our universe in its construction. Our world is layered in dimensions. Within these layers exist spirit beings, time and space, and worlds beyond. During ceremony, these layers overlap, and all exist within the human realm. Our prayer items not only act as communication between us and the k'ixinai but also keep us grounded in this world. Hai K'ise:qot, a head piece that drapes down the back, is adorned with a prayer painted in intricate designs for the K'ixinai that are standing behind the dancers. Blue jay, dove, and other tail feathers of blessed birds are intricately tied at the bottom of a k'ise:qot to enhance the delivery of the prayer and to sweep the energy following the dancer as he moves in a spiritual way. An eagle feather sits above and carries the vibration of the prayers out and beyond. I have had the opportunity to create and recreate many of these things. Each regalia piece has a specific and unique purpose. A regalia maker understands and becomes accountable to the prayer. . . .

• ✦ •

In the summer of 2018, during the Jump Dance of the Yurok people, I stood waiting for the dancers to come up the river from Cate village, toward Pecwan where the Sragon Dancers were dancing. Until recently, Joe Jerry's Dance Camp had not come out for approximately ninety years. Although it was talked about often over the years to bring this side out, the dance-makers waited for a leader or leaders with the right characteristics to lead this camp, and also to have enough regalia to support this revitalized camp. Six years previously, Jake Blake and Frankie Masten, both young men, had been selected. It was one of the most beautiful sites I was privileged to witness. In the distance, I could see the eleven feathers atop the dancer's heads, gently vibrating in the wind. The dancers walked in single file. The Me:wh nasita:n (headdress) shone a brilliant red in the afternoon sunlight. Adorned in old dentalium necklaces, faces painted, and wrapped in xoji-teh (deer-skin blankets) they moved with careful steps. Walt, the mah-chi-qal (one who walks in front) moved toward the dance house with his cane guiding his steps. Each dancer mindful of his purpose. Some silently mumbled in prayer. As the line passed, I saw the things I had made. I was overwhelmed at the beauty of the kisiqot, beads, blankets, and young men who wore them. At the end of the line, Jake and Frankie followed. I smiled quietly to myself. Four of the me:w nasita:n I had worked on for a long period of time were among them. The gathering, care and attention given to the spirit animals and materials was worth the many years in prayer with my ancestors.

Although I'd like to continue with the stories of whił dinił'ay, I will end with saying that knowledge of our ancestors is not always easy to find—and shouldn't be. There are so many lessons in the process of regalia making. A regalia maker understands the complex network in our world. We often open ourselves up to historical trauma, struggle to maintain the integrity of our way, and have a continual struggle to qualify ourselves and our traditions. For me, there has been healing in the making of prayer items, genetic memory vs. epigenetics. I am a regalia maker with a passionate relationship to the implicit nature of our environment and to the timeless prayers. When I look at ceremonial regalia I see myself, my people, and our way of life. I am reminded who I am. "I am you and you are the other me" (Le Red). We as "spiritual beings on a human journey" continually seek those within that come out and are born again.

About This Story

These pieces by Callie Lara appear in *Ka'm-t'em: A Journey Toward Healing*, a book we picked up at the Prairie Creek Visitor Center that quickly became one of our favorites among those we brought home. A collection of writing from Indigenous authors, the book aims to share "Indigenous knowledge, the journey to protect it, and the healing that occurs through transmitting it to younger generations" and to inspire "reclamation of identity, and encourage readers to seek, search, embrace and value their own truth." Lara was a regalia maker, storyteller, writer, teacher, and member of the federally recognized Hoopa Valley Tribe with Karuk ancestry dedicated to revitalizing ceremony and traditional ways of life for Native people along the Redwood Coast.

"Songs of 'Those Within'" shows us Lara's deep connection with the materials she gathered and the power of ceremony and tradition. "'I Am a Visitor of the Forest'" reminds us that we are a part of nature, not above or outside of it, and not entitled to take from it—and that when we do, it's important to show respect and remember we are guests, even if we consider the forest home. Lara's writing provides a window into the traditions of the Hupa people, and it gave us a new appreciation for the regalia we saw at the Trinidad Museum. These are incredible objects of art in themselves, but their meaning for those who make, wear, and witness them in ceremony comes alive through Lara's words.

Hiking the Skunk Cabbage Trail

DAVID HOLPER

We go as gift to one another,
on our anniversary: we last hiked this way
nearly twenty years before. Now, a little older
a little slower, we start late,
with no mind to the eight-mile trip
that lies before us. We eagerly wend our way
up the valley. July is almost over,
and the chrome yellow flowers
of the skunk cabbage are passed.
The light is as green as memory
under the giant Sitka spruce:
talking of building the trail
talking of our life together. Evidence
of logging is everywhere
we look. Now red alder
has filled in the gaps left by the fallen
redwoods. Then the climb begins:
first the switchbacks up the valley wall;
later, the ramp that leads over the ridge,

delivering us after a long stretch
on Gold Bluff's Beach. There,
you take off your shoes, your socks,
your pants and wade out into the waters.
For as far as the eye can see, there is no one
to watch this baptism. Nor any need for any eye
except mine. For this, my love, is the gift
of what time in all its slow certitude
has no sway.

Hejira

DAVID HOLPER

Just after the summer solstice, I hike to see
the tallest tree in the world. I come thinking, I suppose,

of myself: of the story I will tell or the splendid photos
I will share. Hiking up the creek though, I lose myself

in the cold clear water, the lazy scooting of the green frogs
who kick and swim away unafraid before my feet. The light echoes

that same green and sweeps away whatever foolish ideas
or worries I have borne with me. I climb over and under

the fallen trees along the creek, balancing on the moss
covered way, careful to keep my footing, careful

to do no harm. I lose my breath, I lose my way, wandering
up a false trail, thinking I have arrived. Resigning myself

to failure, I hesitate, winded. Then, without thinking,
I let the forest draw me over one more fallen tree,

and the way magically opens. I ascend the hill above
where the ancient giant stands. At its base, you cannot see

just how tall the tree really is. Which is just as well. It is just
a giant among other giants, but it is enough

to show how small a thing I am. I stand there growing smaller
for a great while, thinking of the centuries this tree has stood

here—and I am left thinking of how it will stand long after I am gone.
And larger still the sky, the universe bending down upon me. I breathe

in the rich air the forest offers. Then I silently give thanks to be
in the presence of such magnificent living beings

before I hike back to my truck and climb into the self
that so easily forgets such vastly important things.

About This Story

We first got in touch with writer, poet, and teacher David Holper on a detective mission—trying to track down a poet featured in an anthology he was involved in editing. We were unsuccessful in reaching that poet, but David offered to spread the word to local writing groups, including the poetry group that meets at his house, and sent over work of his own for us to consider. His poetry immediately hooked us, bringing us along on two hikes we think many readers will want to walk in person rather than just read about.

In the summer of 1988, David worked as the director of the Young Adult Conservation Corps (YACC) in Redwood National Park, where he led two crews of young folks from Arcata and Crescent City in completing the last section of the Skunk Cabbage Trail before it was opened to the public that summer. This trail, part of the California Coastal Trail system, is a full sensory experience for those looking for something other than redwoods, offering the feel of wind off ocean waves and the sounds and scents of Douglas-fir and Sitka spruce trees left untouched by logging companies that have thrived in their place and now tower above.

David's other piece, "Hejira," reminds us of the beauty to be experienced en route to a destination and the awe these ancient giants stir when we stand below them. When David first sent us this piece, the title and text mentioned the name of the tree he hiked to, but he removed the name to honor a request made by several scientists we interviewed along the Redwood Coast, who shared concern that anthropomorphizing the trees by naming them was causing them harm. Enticed by images on social media, people were often using the GPS coordinates of named trees to trek off trail to capture their own images of them, causing damage to the redwoods' shallow roots and understory.

Journey to Kronos

RICHARD PRESTON

Excerpt from *The Wild Trees*

When I first met Steve Sillett, he mentioned that the top of Kronos, a tree that stands at the west end of the Atlas Grove, had broken off and was resting against the top of Rhea, beside Zeus, the tallest member of the Atlas Grove. In Greek mythology, the Titan Kronos was the father of Zeus and the god of time. Eventually, the broken top of Kronos had slipped loose from Rhea and calved to the forest floor. Broken limbs and pieces of shattered buttresses had rained down through both trees, leaving widow-makers and hangers suspended throughout their crowns. The event may also have left debris hanging in Zeus—no one knew, because nobody had dared to climb up and try to find out. The calving event left a tangle of rigging lines jammed in the trees crowns, mixed with pieces of defunct scientific gear.

Two years after the top of Kronos fell, a strong winter storm hit Prairie Creek Redwoods State Park and knocked over several large redwoods. The storm did further damage to Kronos and Rhea.

The west end of the Atlas Grove had been abandoned by researchers for years. In the winter of 2006, Sillett and Antoine decided to enter the area, explore it, and remove the damaged rigging and scientific gear as well as all other traces of human presence. “I don’t like to see techno-trash stuck up in redwoods,” Sillett said. They asked me to come with them. We would try to restore the trees to a wild state, and after that they would not be climbed again.

Since Rhea and Kronos were full of concealed debris, the best way to get into them, it seemed, was to climb up Zeus and then attempt to skywalk across the top of the canopy into them. “We’re going to go over to Rhea and Kronos from the top and climb down through them, so we won’t be exposed to something falling on us from above,” Sillett explained to me.

Movement from tree to tree is called an aerial traverse. A climb that proceeds in multiple aerial traverses horizontally through a canopy is called a canopy trek. In canopy trekking, you pull your ropes and gear along with you as you skywalk through a forest, leaving nothing behind. We would carry very little rope, and the least amount of gear possible, so that we could move fast and lightly.

• ✦ •

On the morning of our planned canopy trek, rains were predicted with high winds; the weather radar showed that a storm front was moving in from the Pacific Ocean.

“I’m not a wuss,” Marie Antoine said. “Well, I’m somewhat of a wuss. But I’m ready to climb today.”

We bushwhacked into the Atlas Grove carrying our gear. It began to drizzle, and the sky got very dark. The ground at the west end of the grove was choked with freshly fallen limbs, buttresses, and branches, mixed in with fresh green foliage. Much of the debris had fallen from Rhea and Kronos within the past few weeks, and some might also have come from Zeus—we couldn’t tell.

"We'll just have to see what the situation is when we get up there," Sillett said, peering up into the spaces among the trees.

We pulled a rope into Zeus. Nobody had climbed Zeus since the day Sillett and Antoine had gotten engaged there.

As Sillett climbed up the rope, Antoine stood on a log and watched him, holding a radio. The rain began to fall more steadily. The sea was rumbling and groaning beyond a ridge, five miles away. A loud, raw winter sea.

Sillett climbed slowly, with extreme caution. The fresh chunks of redwood that lay on the ground amounted to the largest debris ring I had ever seen. There was no question that the sound of this stuff falling would have carried for a mile or two.

Sillett got near the top of Zeus, and pretty soon two climbing ropes were hanging down, and Antoine and I went aloft. . . .

• ✦ •

Sillett was standing near the top of Zeus, facing Rhea. He walked out on a branch as far as he could, unfurled his long green rope, and flung it toward Rhea. He got the rope draped over a branch in Rhea, dangling down. Then he pulled a grapnel hook from the fly-fishing reel on his saddle and tossed the hook toward the end of the green rope. He snagged the rope and pulled it back to him, then clipped himself to the loop, stepped out into space, and crossed over to Rhea, hanging from a V formed by the blue and green ropes, one anchored in each tree.

Sillett disappeared inside the top of Rhea. We could hear him moving around. "There's a giant hanger here," he called out. He reap-peared, walking along a slender branch nearly out to its tip, dragging a black mass. It was a piece of Kronos. He wrestled it out of the tree and kicked it into space. It landed in the debris ring with a crash.

It was my turn to cross over. Since my spider rope wasn't long enough to carry me from Zeus to Rhea, Silet proposed using his green rope to construct a zipline, a horizontal traverse rope. In order to set up the zipline, I would need to get a line over to him. I was carrying a bag that contained a long yellow throw line with a weighted throw bag on the end of it. I unfurled the line and tossed the bag toward Sillett. It traveled on a high arc, like a pop fly, dragging the line after it, and landed in Sillett's arms.

We used the throw line to establish the traverse rope, and I clipped a pulley to it and bobbed toward Rhea. Halfway across, I stopped and looked down. I was thirty-one stories up, but there was no sense of height: I was hanging a few feet above floorlike masses of greenery.

I came into Rhea and anchored myself to a branch. Sillett untied the zipline and pulled it out of Zeus. It was like casting off a line from a ship. The rope had been our last connection to Zeus and to the main rope leading to the ground. We had gone into motion.

Over in Zeus, the backup climber stretched herself out on a branch. The weather seemed to be improving.

Sillett and I spidered a short way down through the top of Rhea and came into a small, beautiful glade. Rhea had a double top, with twin trunks, and there was a garden between them. Rhea Garden was a deep pocket of soil that had become established near the top of the tree. The pocket was filled with plants, mosses, and lichens. It was like a tiny Japanese garden, and it was probably as old as the Muro-machi tea gardens of Kyoto. It was built up of layers of earth that had drifted into the tree. I did not want to touch it.

A curving redwood branch arched over the garden like a bridge. I branchwalked along the bridge, keeping my weight suspended on my rope as I looked down into the garden. It was enveloped in shade and hidden in the surrounding foliage—a green chamber in the air.

Sillett had disappeared through a hole in the wall of the chamber. "Are you coming?" his voice filtered up through the hole.

I spidered down through the hole, went around a corner, and came out into a canopy canyon, the most spectacular view I had ever seen in the redwood forest. The canopy canyon was a blasted, ruined void between Kronos and Rhea, extending down into darkness. This was where the leaning top of Kronos had fallen. All the buttresses, hanging fern gardens, and huckleberry thickets had been torn off along both trees. What was left was a cleft filled with sunlight. Kronos Chasm. Debris and broken branches were suspended and clinging to both trunks all the way down into the chasm, as far as the eye could see, and there was no sight of the ground.

Sillett was standing sideways in the air with his feet planted on Rhea's trunk, suspended from a spider rope. He took up his radio and spoke to Antoine, who was somewhere out of sight in Zeus. "'Everything is changed up here, Marie."

"I'm not surprised to hear that."

"It's virtually unrecognizable."

I sat down on a branch and tied myself to it using a very short rope. I was feeling dizzy. Below me was nothing but the ruined face of Rhea descending into darkness. In front of me, at eye level, was the sheared-off top of Kronos. It was a broken shell of rotting wood, with an interior that looked like sawdust. A single live branch stuck out of the shell.

Sillett tossed his rope across to Kronos, aiming for the branch at the top. He caught it with his rope, used his grapnel hook to retrieve it, and skywalked over to Kronos. He ended up standing on the branch.

"I can see the whole top of Kronos swaying under your weight," I said.

"What's it doing, vibrating?"

"Yes. I think you should be very careful."

"I'm not worried," he said, adding that if Kronos's top collapsed he could bail out—he could jump and swing back to Rhea on the green rope. "Do you want to come over here?"

"I think I'll stick to Rhea," I said.

He nodded and swung himself down below the branch so that he was hanging from it on his blue spider rope. He peered into a hole in the top of Kronos and took out his radio. "Oh, my goodness," he said. "This top is totally hollow. I can see all the way down through the middle of the trunk. We've found a rotten shell here."

Antoine's voice came over the radio: "Steve, I don't want you taking chances. Kronos is truly crumbling."

The rotten top of Kronos was crisscrossed with threadlike roots. A coast redwood seems to have the ability to send out roots from any part of its tissue, including its top. Kronos may be putting roots into its own dead top, and feeding on its own decay—as if a person who was dying of gangrene were able to get nutrients from his rotting flesh, and thereby keep himself alive somewhat longer. . . .

• ✦ •

At a hundred and seventy feet, I stood on the lowest branch of Rhea. It was an epicormic branch—a dog's hair branch, ready to be shed by the tree at some point—but I thought that it felt solid. The trunk of Kronos stood about forty feet away. Sillett was hanging in midair across from me, suspended from his spider rope, which was anchored over a lump of bloated gnarl as big as a sofa, which bulged out of Kronos above him.

"Why don't you come over here?" he said.

My spider rope wasn't long enough to reach across the space.

He threw me the end of his green rope, and it landed in a spray of small branches ten feet below me. I got out my grapnel hook and fished up the rope, clipping it to my harness. Then I looped my spider rope over the epicormic branch, hung my weight on it, and stepped out into space away from Rhea, hanging on a V of ropes between the two trees as I skywalked across Kronos Chasm. I ended up dangling in my harness in the air next to Sillett.

"You realize that you placed your life on an epicormic branch," he said.

"It was solid. Anyway, you've been known to do it."

We rested, getting ready for the final move, which would be downward through Kronos. The rain and the wind had stopped. The storm had never come. "We got a gift," Sillett said.

I could see Marie Antoine across from us, hanging in the air along Zeus. "The light's going," she reminded us.

Silett didn't seem ready to go down. He was silent for a while. I could tell that these trees had a personal meaning for him. We were hanging within sight of the tree where he and his wife had declared their love for each other and had planned their future together. We were surrounded by the trees of the Atlas Grove, the center of his career as a botanist and a place in which he had risked his life many times. "There's always a moment during a climb when you lose yourself," he said. "You don't have a name anymore. When you find yourself in a place in nature where if you make a mistake you will die, you become open to what's around you. You start feeling the limits of your perceptions as a human being. You perceive time more clearly in redwoods, and you see time's illusory qualities."

We were looking down into a vast bowl of ferns out of which the three titans grew. "When you feel one of these trees moving, you get a sense of it as an individual," Sillett said

"Do you really think of a tree as a kind of entity?" I asked.

"It's a being. It's a 'person,' from a plant's point of view. A tree is not conscious, the way we are, but it has a perfect memory. This is because the trunk of a tree continually records everything that happens to it as it grows. Plants are very different from us, but they begin life the same way we do, with a sperm and an egg. People think of trees as objects, just something by the side of the road, like a rock. Trees are responsive and alive. They react more slowly than we do, but see how intricate they become. Kronos started from a seed as big as a fingernail clipping, and it did this."

We were surrounded by buttresses, platforms, and Gothic towers, reaching out of sight. The Atlas Grove is believed to be the oldest grove of redwoods on the planet, and we were aloft in what is thought to be its oldest part. Zeus Tree may have been alive when the worship of the god was strong in the cities of Hellas.

"There is a larger issue," Sillett went on. "The redwood forests of California were the most beautiful forests on earth, and they're almost totally gone. They were reduced to scraps by us. Our society—and I don't mean just American society; I mean Chinese, Brazilian, European society, all of us as humans—we are homogenizing the earth's biosphere. We don't know what will happen to the biosphere or to the forests. I'm afraid that our work trying to understand the redwood forest might just turn out to be documenting something magnificent before it winks out. This forest gives us a glimpse of what the world was like a very long time ago, before humans came into existence. We are in one of the last great rain forests remaining in the temperate zone. These tiny little pockets are all that's left of it. We can talk about conserving biodiversity, conserving species, but that isn't enough. We could keep the redwood species alive as a bunch of little redwood trees, but this forest and all that it shows us would be gone.

"What does it show us?"

"Maybe these trees can teach us something about ourselves. Marie and I and you, we're nothing. We're little snapshots in time, and we'll soon be gone. This grove has burned in huge fires during the past millennia. Redwoods don't die if they burn. A redwood can be burned to a blackened spar, and afterward it goes, 'Wooah, and just grows back. Look at Kronos. It's been hammered. It's dying. And it's more beautiful than ever. These trees can teach us how we can live. We can be hammered and burned, and we can come back and be more beautiful as we grow." He paused. "Dude, it's getting dark. We need to go down."

• ✦ •

We dropped down into a maze of standing trunks of all sizes. It was an aerial grove of redwoods that rise out of a buttressed platform extending from the side of Kronos, the largest trunk complex growing from a limb that has yet been identified on a redwood. It was the Great Kronos Complex, otherwise known as Kronos Wood. It had twenty-two trunks in it, springing out of a huge mass that grew sideways from the tree's main trunk. The platform extended for sixty feet out of the side of Kronos. The bigger "trees" in Kronos Wood were between eighty and a hundred feet tall and up to a yard and a half across at their bases. The largest of them was bigger than the Red Queen, the biggest tree in my woods.

We descended through Kronos Wood, spidering down along different trunks and pulling tape and tags off as we went. Kronos Wood was a fractal maze of redwoods springing from redwoods.

It reminded me of a remark by the physicist Eugene Wigner, who said that the fact that nature seems to know mathematics is a wonderful gift that we neither understand nor deserve.

We ended up standing in a bed of earth and ferns on the floor of Kronos Wood. We tidied up the place, taking out the salamander lodges. Then Sillett stepped into the air and disappeared, rappelling down into the tops of some very tall hemlock trees that were not tall enough to reach the base of Kronos Wood.

"Oh!" his voice rang up.

"What is it, Steve?" Antoine asked.

"My rope isn't long enough. I haven't reached the ground."

He was dangling at the very end of his longest rope, twenty feet above the forest floor.

I leaned out. "What are you going to do?"

No answer. Clinking sounds. A minute later, he said, "I'm on the ground." He had clipped his short spider rope to the longer one, creating a daisy chain. The chain had touched the ground, and he had gone down along it.

I would be the last person to see Rhea Garden and Kronos Wood for a long time, if ever again. Sillett had removed all the climbing aids from the trees. He and Antoine intended never to climb in the west end of the Atlas Grove in their lifetimes, and they intended that no one else would, either. The trees would be left to go wild.

About This Story

Richard Preston is a science writer who has written books about infectious disease, bioterrorism, and redwoods. In an author's note prefacing his beloved book *The Wild Trees*, Preston writes, "So many incredible things happen in our world that are never noticed, so many stories never get told. My goal is to reveal people and realms that nobody had ever imagined." The resulting book gives a fascinating look at one of the most unique research labs ever to inquire into the science of redwoods.

Preston discovers this science by shadowing Stephen Sillett, a botanist who teaches at Cal Poly Humboldt and who has dedicated much of his career to the field study of giant sequoia, Douglas-fir, Sitka spruce, and coast redwoods. In fact, Stephen met his wife, Marie, while pioneering this type of work, and they got married in a redwood tree. "The problem was," they recalled, "to find a minister who could climb a redwood." With a gift for explaining the trees' complex biology, Preston tells how research has uncovered that redwoods are both male and female, can come back from fire, and can take in moisture through their needles and feed on the fog in the sky.

In a second preface, Preston explains that botanists "have a tradition of never revealing the exact location of a rare plant. Contact between humans and rare plants is generally risky for the plants." This illustrates an inherent tension in the preservation of redwoods. Though the desire to ascribe human characteristics to trees and name them can be strong, doing so feeds a culture that is often harmful to the trees. For as mighty and resilient as redwoods are, they are also sensitive to changes to their understory and have shallow roots that can deteriorate with too many footsteps. Naming trees has contributed to a rush of visitation to certain redwoods.

We struggled with our decision to include this story. On one hand, it is a gripping tale that reveals the secret world that exists at the tops of the redwoods. On the other hand, the story identifies three named trees. Ultimately, we thought the arc of the story and its conclusion, where the scientists remove all climbing apparatus in an effort to rewild these trees, align with the contemporary attitude toward the conservation of trees. To protect these redwoods, we must not make any one tree famous. Our very forest depends on it.

At the Center of the Earth

TOLOWA DEE-NI' NATION

With the ocean to the west, the majestic ancient redwoods to the east, and rivers filled with fish, Del Norte County is located within the Taa-laa-waa-dvn, the ancestral territory of the Tolowa people. The southern portion of Tolowa territory is on the redwood-studded coastline of the scenic Pacific Ocean in Northern California and is truly one of the most beautiful places on earth.

We citizens of Tolowa Dee-ni' Nation are known as Tolowa Dee-ni' (Tolowa citizen) or Xvsh (human beings). Our ancestral lands, or Taa-laa-waa-dvn, lay along the Pacific Coast within the watersheds of Daa-ghestlh-ts'a' Taa-ghii~-li~ (Wilson Creek) and Xaa-wan' Taa-ghii~-li~ (Smith River) in California, and Duu-srxuu-shi' Taa-ghii~-li~ (Winchuck River), Chit-xu Taa-ghii~-li~ (Chetco River), Ch'vt-le'sr-chvn-dvn Taa-ghii~-li~ (Pistol River), Yaa~-shuu-chit Taa-ghii~-li~ (Rogue River), K'vms-me' Taa-ghii~-li~ (Elk River), and Ts'aa-xwii-chit (Sixes Rivers), extending inland throughout the Taa-xuu-me' Taa-ghii~-li~ (Applegate River) in Oregon. Taa-laa-waa-dvn roughly covers what are today Curry, Josephine, and Del Norte Counties, and encompasses more than

100 miles of coastal shoreline and approximately 2.87 million square acres of land and an undefined acreage of marine waters in Northern California and southern Oregon. These watersheds and lands constitute our place of origin and our continued habitation and occupancy, demonstrated by the ancestral villages of our people within these boundaries.

Taa-laa-waa-dvn is comprised of eleven traditional *yvtlh-'i~* (governance districts). Traditionally, each district was governed distinctly, overseen by a *xvsh-xay-yu'* (headman) who was responsible for making decisions that would best serve the district and the Tolowa living within it. The *xvsh-xay-yu'* was usually the wealthiest and most respected man in the district. Wealthiest, meaning that they were responsible for the care of their *yvtlh-'i~*, upholding traditional laws, providing food and cultural materials for ceremonial purposes, and making payments to settle grievances. There are strict and direct protocols and practices that demand attention as they relate to every institution (land, water, food, people) that embodies our worldview as Indigenous people. Strong hearts and courageous leadership are the driving characteristics of the *xvsh-xay-yu'* of historical and current periods.

Traditionally, Tolowas lived in redwood plank homes set into the earth with clay, stone, wood, and cordage. These dwellings have distinctive central peaks and rounded entrance doors, and they reflect a profound connection to our environment and our rich cultural heritage. Integral to our culture is a deep reverence for all living beings, guided by the belief that everything possesses a spirit and purpose, highlighting a spiritual harmony with the natural world.

We have a reciprocal relationship with the *k'vsh-chu* (redwoods). Our genesis narrative explains how they were created at Yan'-daa-k'vt, the Center of the World, where a white redwood tree stood. At creation, we were instructed:

"K'wa'-lee-shvm 'aylh-nvn, "Xwii-day 'uu-xu'lh-te wvn k'ee-naa-ch'u'-'a. K'wan'-lee-shvm xwii-day nayslh-sri~. Xwii-day see waa nays-'a~." "Pray for everything you need."

and

"Dii nvn-'e lhinlh-sa'-dvn shaa~ k'vsh-chu xvm-num-ni. Hii dii-ta waa wee-ni yvslh-'a~. Hii-waa-sha~." "At the center of this earth is the only place the redwoods came to grow. In this earth it is kept this way. That's all of it."

Integral to our culture are enduring values of self-responsibility, community, and environmental stewardship. Renowned as skilled hunters and gatherers, we employ redwood oceangoing dugout canoes for travel, gathering bird eggs, and hunting seals and sea lions. Today, we continue to source a diverse array of sustenance from the land and sea, including a variety of seaweed, shellfish, fresh and saltwater fish, deer, berries, elk, tea, and acorns. We also recognize and respect the nutritional significance and ancestral ties of eating, gathering, and harvesting traditional foods. Central to our identity is our intimate relationship with the land, from which we derive vital resources. Gathering medicinal herbs and basketweaving materials, we continue to uphold traditional practices and ways of knowing passed down to us by our ancestors.

Our history bears witness to profound challenges and resilience. Euro-American contact precipitated a series of devastating events, including the destruction of villages, loss of land, forced displacement, erosion of traditional culture, and the second largest act of genocide in American history. Following the upheaval wrought by the gold rush era, which saw many tribes decimated, we persevered, preserving our cultural heritage through adversity. Despite enduring trauma, genocide, termination, and population decline—reflected bluntly in the precipitous drop from an estimated ten thousand individuals to just over one hundred by 1910—we persisted, reclaiming federal recognition and establishing a sovereign tribal government, the Tolowa Dee-ni' Nation.

Despite these challenges, we endure, maintaining ancestral practices and forging a path forward. Understanding and respecting our history and culture offers invaluable insights for visitors to the region. From the governance structures to understanding the boundaries of Taa-laa-waa-dvn to the enduring connections with the land and its resources, our cultural legacy is an integral part of the fabric of the Pacific Northwest region. Through preservation efforts and intergenerational practices, we continue to uphold our rich heritage, ensuring that our story is shared for generations to come.

Visitors to the region are encouraged to explore our legacy of Indigenous stewardship in shaping the landscapes. Despite the draw of the region's robust beauty—embracing mountains, free-flowing rivers, redwood forests, and ocean beaches—it is imperative to acknowledge the foundational role of our people in conserving and maintaining these lands. We encourage visitors to learn about our rich history and cultures. We hope that you share our history as a way of acknowledging and honoring the people who came before you. Wherever you go, please visit respectfully and responsibly.

About This Story

We were honored to connect with the Tolowa Dee-ni' Nation and work with Emily Reed, the Nation's Administrative Services Director, who was instrumental in creating this piece about the Tolowa people for this collection. The Tolowa Dee-ni' Nation of more than two thousand citizens is a federally recognized tribe with headquarters located 3 miles south of the Oregon-California border. The seven-member tribal council established in 1987 is the governing body of the Nation pursuant to its constitution. The government's executive director and staff operate according to a framework of codes, policies, and committees created by resolution of the tribal council. All of the Nation's decisions are based on time-honored cultural values and contemplate the best interests of future Tolowa Dee-ni' generations.

The tribe's younger generation is interested in using the power of storytelling to educate the public and give their side of the story. Many nonnative versions of their story, Emily told us, are shared broadly and even taught in schools, perpetuating inaccuracies and racism that still exists today. The tribe's history and connection to the redwoods are key elements to convey, as these majestic trees are often what draw people to this region, and historically the Indigenous narrative has been absent from these places. Today, when you visit the Grove of Titans in Jedediah Smith Redwoods State Park, part of Redwood National and State Parks in Del Norte County, you can read new interpretive signage that was developed in partnership with representatives of the Tolowa Dee-ni' Nation.

When I Grow Up

HARRY K. ROBERTS

Excerpt from *Walking in Beauty: Growing Up with the Yurok Indians*

The wind was soft on our skins as we lay half hidden in the marsh grass and watched the river otters playing on the clay slide in our swimming hole. We had gathered many thimbleberry leaf baskets of salmon berries and were eating them while the sun dried us off.[1] It was one of those soft, warm, quiet days when the Mayflies dance and you can hear the earth hum.

I called my friend "Hi-pur" because he always played outways from the earth center at Kenek.[2] Whenever I went to find him at his home his grandmother pointed to Oregos, the great rock that guards the mouth of the river, and said *hipur*, which meant that he was down on the ocean beach learning about the ocean things. He usually called me *herkwer*, rabbits, like Roberts.

This day we had taken the canoe up the river into one of the sloughs that was in the spruce swamp to go swimming and to get salmon berries. We were all full of nice swim and fresh salmon

1 The thimbleberry bush has wide, soft, plant leaves. These were fashioned into small containers secured with twigs for collecting, in this case, salmon berries.

2 Hi-pur (hipur) is a directional term meaning "northward; toward the river mouth; down below." (Thomas Buckley)

berries and life was very good, and we talked of how we would like to be when we grew up.

Hi-pur said he would be a great hunter like his younger uncle and he would know all about how to be hunting all kinds of animals and fishes, and he would always keep a great big smokehouse full of smoked fish and deer and elk and especially smoked sturgeon, which is the best of all. But he didn't know if he could be a great hunter and a Man because there were no longer any sweathouses to make the early morning prayer fire.

I was going to study to know the law and I would go far back into the mountains to make my medicine to be a man like our elder uncle, and I would marry Hi-pur's sister and we would all live together in our family house.

So we lay in the sun and watched the otters play and spun our dreams of how it might be when I could walk with the spirits and find the deer and fish for him to catch so that we would have plenty of food. We thought of how it was that we should know if we could speak with the spirits and see the meaning of things, and if we were strong enough to face Creation and accept the law. We should have to put ourselves to the test all of the time.

The first test we could think of was to feel like a redwood tree and to see if our canoe would listen to us. So we spent the afternoon trying to think like a tree. Then we took turns with the canoe to see who it would behave best for. Hi-pur ran the canoe every which way like a log in the ocean. He finally got caught in a snag and we had to swim to get the canoe free. He said that he could talk to the ocean and he should stay off of the river where he couldn't make his canoe listen to him.

I pounded on the side of the canoe with my paddle handle until I could make a canoe-tree song. The canoe danced over the water and between the snags and my feet grew into the foot-rests and

Hi-pur said he could not tell us apart as the canoe looked like me and I looked like part of the canoe, and it must be that I was able to talk to the spirit that was in the canoe, and maybe it was because I came from the beforetime people. We both thought that this might be because the redwood tree was a man in the beforetime. This is how it happened:

In the early days when it was that the Wo-gay lived here there was a very fine, big, strong man who lived right. When all of the world was to be cleaned by the flood this man was so fine and good that Creation took pity on him and said what would be best would be for the man to say what he would like to be after the flood. So the Wo-gay said that he would like to be a big, fine redwood tree for the new human beings to make houses and canoes of. So that is how it is that a canoe has a heart and a main artery and a face and a nose and a place for a necklace and why it wears a hat and a necklace.[3] And you can sing and talk to that spirit and the canoe will sing and talk with you, and you skim and dance over the river like so lovely.

3 These are all traditional design features of the Yurok carved redwood canoe, still being made on the river today. (Thomas Buckley)

Jump Dance Song

HARRY K. ROBERTS

Excerpt from *Walking in Beauty: Growing Up with the Yurok Indians*

One time Hi-pur and his brother and sisters and I were playing rock tag on the ocean beach. This tag was to run through the sand and stand on a rock to be safe or, where the beach was mostly rocks, to run over the rocks to a spot of sand.

After we got tired of playing tag we sat on the rocks just above the waves and ate seaweed and Hi-pur talked to the sea lions and they swam up to talk to us. After a while the girls got tired of this and gathered some wood and went home. We boys stayed and had a barking contest with the sea lions.

After a while there were a few candle fish washed up on the beach and we caught them. There were only a few so we went up to the house for some fire and told Grandmother for them not to worry; we would eat on the beach. We made our fire and watched the sunset and ate candlefish and seaweed and acorn bread and sweet grass. We thought to keep the fire burning so the people would know where we were and not worry about us, and we could run up and down the beach kicking the wet sand to see the sparks the phosphorous made. When we got tired we went back to our fire and cooked some more candlefish and sat by the fire listening to what the ocean was saying. But the ocean got very quiet and didn't talk to us. Finally I got a feeling that I should go to one side away from the fire and sit and look at Oregos.[1] So I told Hi-pur what I was going to do and for him to keep the fire going.

I went to where I felt it was to be the place to stop and I sat there very quietly wondering why I should feel that I should do this. After a while I heard a noise among the rocks at the base of Oregos, and finally I heard it clear that some people sang the Jump Dance song there. I walked up closer to the rocks, but then the singing stopped. Then I went back to where I had been, and they sang again, clear and loud. I made a sign for my friend to come over, but when he got to me they stopped their song again.

We didn't know what it meant, so we went home very fast. We were not frightened—we were simply very cautious—and it seemed appropriate that we leave at once as it was getting late and the people might worry about us.

It took us several days to get up courage enough to see Elder Uncle about what I had heard. Uncle was a very great man; he was more than a man; he was one who could "walk in beauty" and speak with the spirits. This thing I had heard was not to be taken lightly—it could be very dangerous or very good for me, I didn't know. Neither of us had ever been told of such a thing happening.

We decided that since I was the one who had heard the song, I should go to Uncle alone, since whatever it was was obviously for me alone, as it stopped when Hi-pur came near. I asked Uncle if anyone ever heard singing at night among those rocks and he said yes. It was the Little People who were making a jump dance

1 Oregos (o regos, Tucker's Rock) is a very large rock, now partially fallen, on the north side of the mouth of the Klamath River, one of the two sisters stationed on either side of the river's mouth to guard it.

because the people had been talking about having a jump dance at Rekwoi but hadn't gotten around to making that dance. And the Little People who owned the jump dance got tired of waiting and were putting on their own dance. It comes about in this way:

In the days before the flood when the people were bad, some of the people were good. These people made themselves very little (about twelve to eighteen inches high) and rode out the flood on bundles of sticks and bulrushes. Creation saw these people do this and asked them why they were trying to stay. The Little People said that it was so they could teach the new people how to make the world-renewing prayer and songs of the jumping dance. So Creation rained on them and washed all of their color out so they could not be seen. That is how we can't see them but only hear them. When there is a jump dance they always come and guard their songs and if there is an impure dancer they make him very sick so he can't dance. If the people don't make the world-renewing prayer then the Little People make the dance themselves, and if some person hears their songs then it is a good dance and the world is renewed in peace. But if no one hears it, their song, then it is bad times are for the world. The jump dance is for prayers that then people should keep the Law and have good thoughts and be pure.

I asked Uncle what it meant that I heard this singing. Then he told me that it was that I could hear the spirits and it would be good for me to make my medicine in the high mountains. He said that when a boy heard this, this is what it meant for him to do. When a grown person hears the songs it just means that they are good and pure, and that they should make a prayer and cast tobacco on their fire. The Little People will know and watch over them and they will be lucky.

So that is how I knew that I was to make my medicine in the high places and to become a Man and to learn the Law.

• ✦ •

Harry's Commentary

About these world-renewing dances: When a dance was put up everyone was happy and excited over going to the dance, for they would see old friends and sing old songs and sing new songs and meet new friends. The young men combed their hair until it shined bright as polished ebony and they wrapped their braids in their best sea otter bands. The young women gathered Sweet Herb and packed it in their hair so that their lovers would smell the perfume as they whispered, one to the other, during the breaks in the dances.

This was the time when we expressed our appreciation to the Spirit of Creation for having made the universe, when the old men sang the songs in the high language that speaks only in emotions, not in words. This was when we showed our best things, feathers, dentalia, medicine baskets or great obsidian blades and the sacred deerskins, the deep blue ones and the pure white ones. These things were held forth in the dance as we thanked Creation for all of everything and showed that we were proud, and not selfish in the face of Creation.

About These Stories

Harry K. Roberts, a young Irish American boy from San Francisco who went on to become a "high man," a trained Yurok spiritual teacher, spent his formative years in the 1910s growing up at the mouth of the Klamath River. Here, his father managed a salmon cannery that employed Native workers, and their family resided in the Yurok village of Requa between spring and fall during the salmon run. The family became close friends with the headman of Requa, Captain Spott, and his son, Robert (Frank) Spott, a spiritual and political leader who became Harry's medicine teacher for more than twenty years, from age eleven to his early thirties. Referred to as Uncle throughout Harry Roberts's book, Robert Spott was highly influential as Harry's mentor, teacher, and counselor.

While we typically avoid sharing Indigenous stories from a non-native perspective, Roberts was trained in a traditional Yurok way of life, and the stories he shares in his book reflect his own memories and experiences of this unconventional upbringing. Thomas Buckley (aka Jōkan Zenshin), whom Roberts became Uncle and teacher to, writes in the book's foreword: "Harry Roberts was a complex man, neither Irish nor Yurok, a lot of both, representing himself as neither. Utterly pragmatic, Harry was also a yarn-spinner and a romantic, and in telling stories from a Native perspective he risks being seen as yet another Ernest Thompson Seton, a co-founder of the Boy Scouts of America. To take him as such would be a mistake. His knowledge ran very deep and was entirely authentic, founded in his earned experience."

The Heartwood Life of Questions

DARYL NGEE CHINN

Listen. Pay attention.
Why are you here?
How long will you stay?

Wait, notice. Wait more.
Wait even more.

Bird, wind, bug, forest.
Earth, fire, air, water.

Cloud, color, breath.
Quiet, flower, trees.

Beach, ocean, chill.
Edge. Middle. Inside.

Trees, water.
Why are they together?
How?

Redwoods, fog.
Madrone, fir, cedar.

Learn the music of names.
Klamath, Baduwa't, Trinity,
Big Lagoon, Stone Lagoon,
Humboldt Bay.

Your people: Who are they?
Why are they here?
What are their stories?

Sequoia, name for redwood.
The deepest, darkest,
and oldest part is heartwood.
The thick bark is the skin.
Heartwood is strong, dead.
What is in your heart?
Do you have thick skin?
What is inside us? Inside you?

Time, with music, live here:
when leaves turn yellow, rustle, and drop.
When warm, long days return.
When dark tree needles grow
light green fingers. When catkins
like lanterns hang on bigleaf maples.

Time flows when water chatters.
Then it lies still, breathless, in the heat.

Salmon swish or leap time.
Time when agates sneak
a place among other stones.

Are you leaving so soon?
Before you leave, learn names,
Wiyot, Tuluwat Island,
learn about Tolowa, Yontoket,
learn gold rush, settler,
learn massacre, the Exclusion,
clear-cut, sneaker wave,
world renewal, ask about
the Brush Dance, ceremonies,
the Indian names, the importance
of the woodpecker, the owl, the raven,
the bear, the basket, the skirts.

Can you learn without asking questions?
What was first, the question or the answer?

Did the idea of tree come before the tree
or did trees gather and say, I will go
toward rain and fog,
close to the crashing waves?

Let others drift and grow. You, too,
grow, change. Talk to each other.

Invent your own words,
learn the old ones,

listen, always listen
as if you were trees, looking
for the best places
to put down roots.

About This Story

Daryl Ngee Chinn's piece feels like a perfect closing meditation on experiencing the redwood forest, whether you visit through the pages of this book or in person. He is a Chinese American poet, teacher, bookmaker, and editor—and served as a founding member of the North Redwoods Book Arts Guild and Humboldt County coordinator for California Poets in the Schools. You can find his work in various collaborative books, self-published chapbooks, and anthologies, and in his own 1989 book *Soft Parts of the Body*.

We learned about Daryl through Humboldt Asians and Pacific Islanders in Solidarity (HAPI), a nonprofit formed in 2021 to honor the history and culture of the first Chinese people in Humboldt County. Wanting to include a story that reflected on this history, we reached out to Daryl to ask if he could create a piece that captured this while also addressing this community's relationship to its natural surroundings. Having been inspired and excited about HAPI's efforts, we were thrilled that Chinn created a piece that's an invitation to move toward a more inclusive and just future. We hope you take a moment to meditate on the important questions his poem poses.

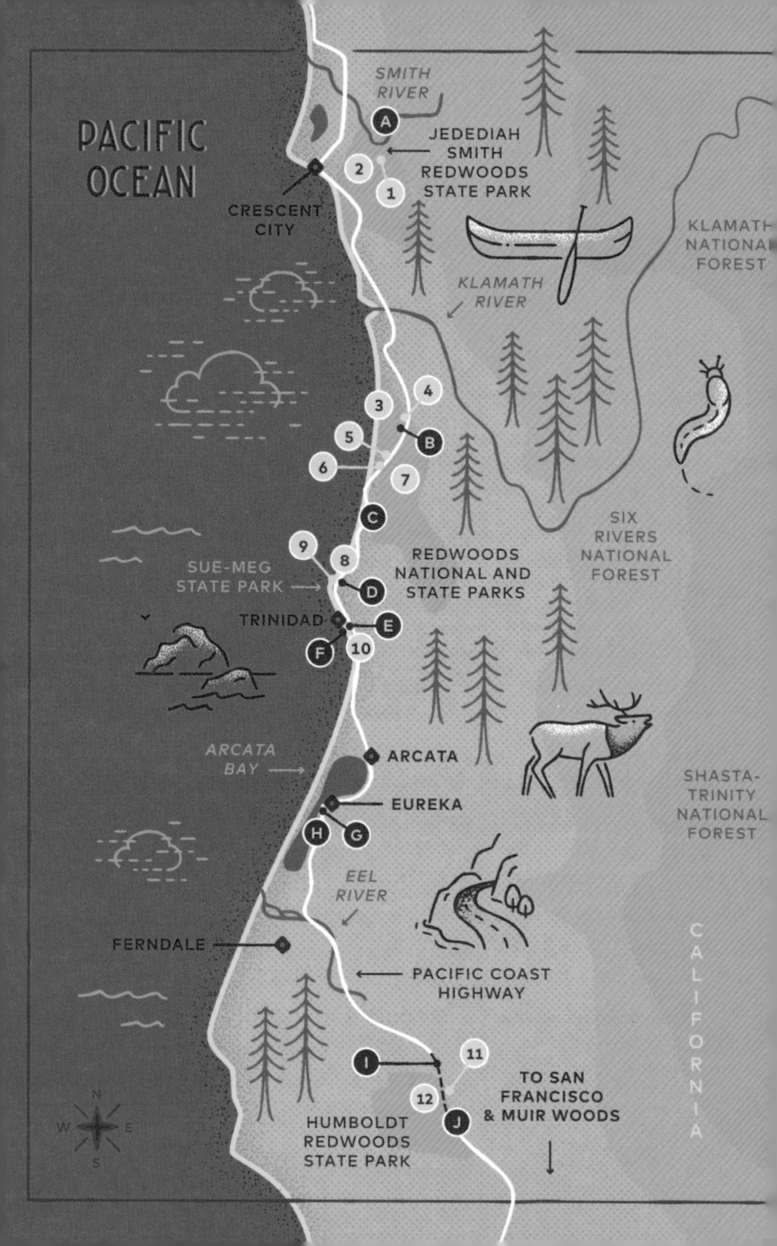
PACIFIC OCEAN
SMITH RIVER
A
JEDEDIAH SMITH REDWOODS STATE PARK
2
1
CRESCENT CITY
KLAMATH NATIONAL FOREST
KLAMATH RIVER
4
3
B
5
6
7
C
SIX RIVERS NATIONAL FOREST
9
8
REDWOODS NATIONAL AND STATE PARKS
SUE-MEG STATE PARK
D
TRINIDAD
E
F
10
ARCATA BAY
ARCATA
SHASTA-TRINITY NATIONAL FOREST
EUREKA
H
G
EEL RIVER
FERNDALE
PACIFIC COAST HIGHWAY
CALIFORNIA
11
I
TO SAN FRANCISCO & MUIR WOODS
12
J
HUMBOLDT REDWOODS STATE PARK
N
W
E
S

EXPLORE

THE REDWOOD COAST

A guide for your next Redwood Coast adventure—on land or water.

ATTRACTIONS

- A Hiouchi Visitor Center
- B Prairie Creek Visitor Center
- C Chah-pekw O' Ket'-toh "Stone Lagoon" Visitor Center
- D Sumêg Village
- E Trinidad Museum
- F Cal Poly Humboldt Marine Laboratory
- G Clarke Historical Museum
- H Historic Eureka Chinatown / Charlie Moon Way
- I Avenue of the Giants
- J Humboldt Redwoods State Park Visitor Center

NATURAL LANDMARKS

1. Stout Grove
2. Grove of Titans
3. Gold Bluffs Beach
4. The Big Tree Loop
5. Trillium Falls Trail
6. Skunk Cabbage Trail
7. Lady Bird Johnson Grove
8. Agate Beach
9. Wedding Rock
10. Luffenholtz Beach
11. Founders Grove
12. Rockefeller Loop

What to Do

Research shows that experiencing a sense of awe is good for your health, so get a dose of nature's best medicine by exploring the many redwood groves and beaches of the North Coast.

Go on a hike under big trees.

Nothing can convey the grandeur of these trees more than walking beneath them. Locals often say the best time to hike through a redwood forest is in the rain, so don't let the weather get you down!

At **Muir Woods National Monument** you'll find a range of trail options for nature lovers of all abilities—from short, accessible paths along Fern Creek and under Cathedral Grove's big trees to longer and more strenuous hikes that lead to views of Mount Tamalpais, the Pacific Ocean, and San Francisco. If you have only a couple hours, we suggest the Fern Creek, Lost, and Canopy Trail Loop. Keep in mind that due to Muir Woods's popularity and proximity to major cities, you'll need to make a parking or shuttle reservation ahead of time.

When you're in **Humboldt Redwoods State Park**, stretch your legs on hikes in Rockefeller Forest and Founders Grove. Or for something farther off the beaten path, take the 4-mile round trip Damnation Creek Trail in **Del Norte Coast Redwoods State Park**, where you'll walk through groves of redwoods and Sitka spruce to a secluded beach worth the effort of navigating the elevation changes.

If you're in **Redwood National Park**, you'll see some really big trees on the aptly named Tall Trees Trail, a moderately strenuous 4.5-mile round trip backcountry hike that requires a permit and descends 800 feet down to Redwood Creek. For an easier hike, the 2.5-mile Big Tree Loop along the Karl Knapp and Cathedral Trees Trails in Prairie Creek Redwoods State Park is a must. For something different, visit the Skunk Cabbage Trail, a nearly 5-mile round trip trail to Gold Bluffs Beach through a shady canyon with alder and, yes, skunk cabbage. The southern trailhead can be accessed off of Highway 101 on Robinson Road, just past the Gold Bluffs Beach entrance kiosk, or use the northern trailhead on Gold Bluffs Beach if you'd like to experience your own "baptism" with a dip in the ocean. The easy Lady Bird Johnson Grove Trail and slightly more moderate Trillium Falls Trail wind their way through verdant forest so thick with alders, big leaf maples, douglas firs, ferns, mosses, trillium, and rhododendron that it feels like you might bump into something extraterrestrial. Just be sure to get a day use permit and reservation if you're traveling in peak season, between mid-May and mid-September.

Take a scenic drive.

You'll find even bigger trees and more rugged coastlines if you travel the historic **Pacific Coast Highway** from Muir Woods up to Crescent City. Stop along the way at coastal seaside destinations like

Point Reyes, Mendocino, and Fort Bragg. You can also drive along the 31-mile **Avenue of the Giants**, rated "the finest forest drive in the world," or the Newton B. Drury Scenic Parkway, both of which wind through the heart of old-growth forests. Or take a day to drive **Howland Hill Road** through our personal favorite stop for big trees on the North Coast, Jedediah Smith Redwoods State Park. (Get out to stroll through the Stout Memorial Grove and the Grove of Titans.)

Get into and onto the water.

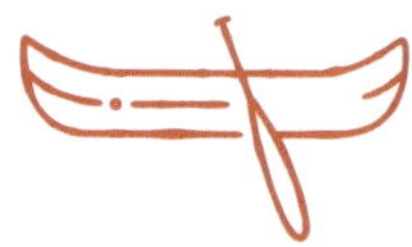

Before planning our own visit to the redwoods, we had no idea how many opportunities there were to get on and into the water! If you're visiting during warmer months, pack swimwear and watershoes to explore the many rivers, streams, beaches, tidepools, dunes, and lagoons. Abundant rivers in the National Wild and Scenic River System flow between trees that stand more than 300 feet high. Consider paddling the clear turquoise waters of the **Smith River** through miles of majestic old-growth forests in the Smith River National Recreation Area. Many outfitters offer guided tours or rentals, and in the summer months, Redwood National and State Parks offer ranger-led kayak tours from the Jedediah Smith Redwoods Day Use Area. In Humboldt Redwoods State Park, you can float the emerald green **Eel River** if you bring your own fishing boat, kayak, canoe, or raft.

For an unforgettable experience, book a guided tour with the Yurok Tribe's Yurok Canoe Tours down the **Klamath River** and hop into one of only three handcrafted traditional dugout redwood canoes available for the public. For a bigger thrill, consider their jet boat tours that zoom you upriver 20 miles. You can also rent kayaks at **Stone Lagoon** from the Indigenous-run Chah-pekw O' Ket'-toh "Stone Lagoon" Visitor Center, which also offers engaging programming and educational displays about the landscape and Indigenous tribes.

If you're looking to cool off on a hot summer day, check out swimming holes along and in **Freshwater County Park** in Eureka, **Mad River Fish Hatchery** in Arcata, **Big Lagoon County Park** near Trinidad, the Smith River in **Jedediah Smith Redwoods State Park**, Redwood Creek in **Redwood National Park**, **Van Duzen County Park** (also known as Swimmers Delight) in Carlotta, or the Eel River in **Humboldt Redwoods State Park**. Or you can visit two of the North Coast's favorite surf spots, **Camel Rock** and **Moonstone Beach** in Trinidad. These breaks have no shortage of good waves, but seasons, currents, swells, and tides—in addition to submerged rocks—can make surfing dangerous, so it's important to do your research ahead of time and check current conditions. (Or maybe just watch from shore.)

Witness wildlife wonders.

Pack your binoculars for an up-close view of the spectacular wildlife all along the rugged Pacific coastline. At any roadside overlook you might see migrating whales or harbor porpoises in the water, seabirds overhead, and seals, California sea lions, Steller sea lions, or northern elephant seals hauled out on the rocks. Your best chance to spot whales is during their migration in the fall and early spring months, and the most common species include gray and humpback whales. If you see a towering dorsal fin and a flash of black and white, you may be one of the lucky ones—killer whales have been spotted

hunting salmon and seals here, too. If you're paddling or exploring the rivers and creeks, you might see a river otter, a species making a triumphant return after a long absence from this region.

Elk can also be spotted near the **Prairie Creek Visitor Center**, on **Gold Bluffs Beach**, and throughout the Orick region. Keep your distance; they are unpredictable and can be dangerous around the fall rut and calving seasons. On the other end of the size spectrum, look for banana slugs when you're among the trees. These bright yellow mollusks, the second largest slug in the world, play an essential part in the health of a redwood forest—they're the cleanup crew, turning leaves, moss, dead plant matter, and animal droppings into a nutrient-rich compost for the redwood forest floor.

Explore rich underwater worlds.

The North Coast has an abundance of intertidal zones teeming with diverse and abundant marine life. Familiarize yourself with the tide tables and plan your day around low tide, when you can visit tidepools and rocks to look for creatures like sea stars, sea urchins, mussels, nudibranchs, hermit crabs, sea anemones, limpets, snails, sea cucumbers, and more. **Old Home Beach** (formerly Indian Beach) in Trinidad and nearby **Palmer's Point Beach** in Sue-meg State Park are two of our favorites. If you're near Crescent City, visit the tidepools along rocky stretches of **Pebble Beach**. Take care not to turn your back to

the ocean and avoid areas with active breaking waves and waves higher than 3 feet.

Didn't pack the right gear, or low tide not working into your itinerary? Stop by Cal Poly Humboldt's **Telonicher Marine Laboratory** in Trinidad, where you can take a self-guided tour of the laboratory and exhibits, featuring several view tanks and a touch tank, to learn more about the region's rich marine ecosystems.

Take in coastal views.

If you're just passing through or you'd rather stay dry and enjoy the coast from a distance, Northern California has no shortage of breathtaking overlooks of rocky coastlines. Don't miss the rocky outcrop at **Trinidad Head**, where you can do a short loop with many lookout points, or visit **Luffenholtz Beach County Park**. If you're in Klamath Country, check out the **Klamath River Overlook** and its spectacular view of the Klamath River draining into the Pacific Ocean, a sacred place for the Indigenous people of Northern California with a long history of traditions.

Wedding Rock in Sue-meg State Park can also be accessed easily by car and a short walk out to the point. While you're there, take a short fern-adorned and mossy trail up to the top of Ceremonial Rock for a different vantage point. Near Muir Woods in the Bay Area, you can take in stunning ocean views at **Muir Beach Overlook**—a relaxing spot to watch the sunset.

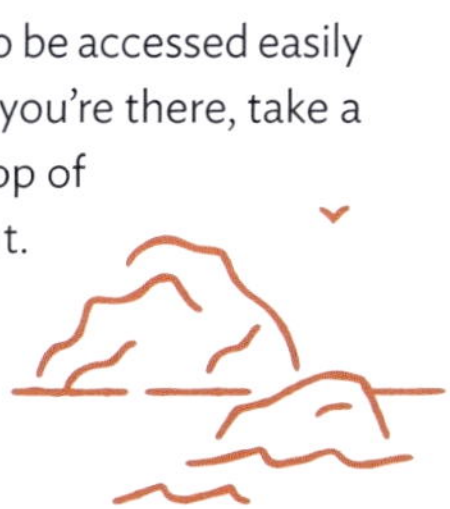

Enjoy the day's catch—or catch your own.

Connection to the ocean, rivers, and streams makes fresh seafood abundant in this region. Enjoy local salmon, trout, and Dungeness

crab at restaurants along the North Coast, which generally offer the season's and day's fresh catch. Dungeness crab season can shift but generally starts in winter and runs through spring or summer depending on conditions. On the move? Be sure to pick up some smoked salmon and salmon jerky at markets and fish houses throughout the region.

If fishing is your thing and you've got the muscles for reeling in a big catch, the region's waterways offer an abundance of fish, including hard-fighting salmon and steelhead in the Smith and Klamath Rivers, as well as salmon, rockfish, and lingcod in the ocean. If you're not booking a trip with one of the many fishing outfitters and private charters, be sure to visit the California Department of Fish and Wildlife website for information on open seasons, allowances and limitations, regulations, and licenses. For something more low key, try fishing and crabbing from **Trinidad Pier**, which sits alongside Little Head Rock. The public is welcome on the privately owned pier as long as you have a fishing license, which you can pick up at **Murphy's Market** in town.

Take in living history and culture.

When you visit the parks and monuments, don't just breeze by the interpretive displays. Take time to learn about the human history of these places. At **Sue-meg State Park**, take the guided or self-guided tour of Sumêg village—a recreated Yurok village intended to be a space for ceremony, education, and healing. Today it's still actively used by the Yurok people and neighboring tribes to preserve and carry on their traditions. You can view Yurok family homes, a sweathouse, changing houses, a redwood canoe, and a dance house, where a three-day Brush Dance is traditionally held. At the **Chah-pekw O' Ket'-toh "Stone Lagoon" Visitor Center**, the first tribally operated visitor center in the California State Parks system, you can learn about the tribe directly from Yurok citizens and their exhibits, and visit the gift shop featuring locally sourced and Indigenous-made gifts.

In July, attend the Tolowa Tribe's dance demonstrations at **Jedediah Smith Campground**. In August, check out the Yurok Tribe's **Klamath Salmon Festival**, where you can see cultural and basket-weaving demonstrations, a parade, stick game and softball tournaments, an axe-throwing competition, kids' activities (including a petting zoo!), a 5k run/walk, and more than a hundred vendors selling food and locally crafted goods. If you're visiting in September, the Tolowa Tribe hosts **Dee'Ni Day**, where you can find cultural demonstrations, local art and food, horseshoe tournaments, stick games, and kids' activities.

The **Clarke Historical Museum** in Eureka focuses on northwestern California history in Humboldt County—including Native Americans, the 1849 gold rush, the logging industry, ranching, farming, and seafaring. Also in Eureka, the **Blue Ox Millworks and Historic Village** will delight handy and crafty folks. Here you can get a glimpse into Victorian craftsmanship in the form of woodworking, ironwork, ceramics, letterpress printmaking, and boat building. The **Trinidad Museum**, in a renovated bungalow home, packs a lot into its five exhibit rooms highlighting Trinidad's natural and cultural history. It also features an impressive display of Yurok regalia made by Trinidad Museum Society board member Shoshoni Gensaw-Hostler, as well as working baskets and ceremonial caps by the Yurok, Karuk, Hoopa, and Wiyot women of northwestern California.

The **Humboldt Redwoods State Park Visitor Center** along the Avenue of the Giants highlights wildlife, fossils, minerals, logging history, Save the Redwoods League, and most peculiarly, the Travel Log, a motor home made from the largest piece of hewn redwood in the world, a hollowed-out 6-ton redwood log mounted on top of a Nash Quad truck. The Travel Log was built by vaudeville entertainer, "nature singer," naturalist, and environmentalist Charles Kellogg, who drove it across the country to bring attention to the redwoods and what was happening to them. In **Founders Grove**, look for the display about Laura Perrott Mahan, a key figure in preserving this museum of living history. Though the grove itself is named for and dedicated to the men of Save the Redwoods League, you can now walk through this magnificent grove and imagine how Mahan put her body between the trees and the machinery.

How to Visit Well

Stay on designated trails.

Though redwood trees have stood mightily for thousands of years through fire, floods, and drought, they live in a complex ecosystem that depends on the health of all living things that surround them in the forest, and their shallow root systems make them especially vulnerable. These forests see millions of visitors each year, so the trails have been designed in a way that allows visitors to be with these giants up close without exposing their roots, trampling their understory, or compacting the soil below, which can create runoff that can spell trouble for spawning salmon and trout.

Protect the natural soundscape.

Here along the Redwood Coast, the natural soundscape of the forest is legally protected in places like Cathedral Grove in Muir Woods, one of the first designated "quiet spaces" in the National Park System. Commercial airplanes are prohibited from flying over Muir Woods, ice machines have been moved, vehicle pull-up zones and parking lots have been shifted away from the visitor centers, and even the cash registers are designed to be quiet. Traditionally, parks calculate the carrying capacity of a space by determining how many people could physically share the trails without feeling crowded, or how many cars fill a parking lot—but it's increasingly recognized that carrying capacity is also about visitors having enough space to enjoy the peace and quiet of the forest, maintaining enough of what the park calls "the natural soundscape" to preserve a primeval experience. It's also about respecting the soundscape needs of denizens of the forest such as the endangered northern spotted owl.

So while you're here, pay attention to the sound of the wind through the branches, the water running through the creek, and birdsong. As you're strolling the redwood groves or enjoying hiking trails with friends and family, be mindful of your volume and the impact you may have not only on other humans' experiences but on the wildlife as well.

Keep it crumb clean!

If you've camped or picnicked along the Pacific Coast, you're probably familiar with the crows, ravens, jays, and magpies that happily wait for you to drop crumbs, share leftovers, or just look away for a few seconds. While their thievery can be an annoyance to us, it can be deadly to the marbled murrelet, a beloved endangered bird that's uniquely adapted to this region and whose eggs in the tops of old-growth trees often fall prey to birds in the Corvidae family. The more trash and crumbs that are left behind, the more these scavenging predator birds learn to hang around this sensitive habitat, making it more difficult for marbled murrelets to survive. That's why the campaign to "Keep It Crumb Clean" is taken seriously here. Whether you're camping, having a picnic, or just snacking along a trail, be sure to pack out trash—down to the very last crumb.

Take care exploring tidepools.

Remember tidepools are homes for living creatures that play an important role in a complex underwater ecosystem. It might be tempting to touch and pick up what you find, but leave tidepool residents alone. Do not overturn rocks, which can damage habitats. Be sure to get an up-close look and take lots of pictures of the rich world of starfish, sea anemones, and hermit crabs to take with you as a souvenir, but leave these critters where they are.

Come prepared and stay aware.

The rugged Pacific coastline is exactly that—rugged, shifting, moving, breathing. Just before we arrived in early spring after a winter of rain, videos on social media were showing giant redwood trees scattered across roads like a game of pick-up sticks and coastal highways washing into the ocean—all par for the course around here. Wind can contribute to trees falling, especially when their shallow roots have been exposed and inundated with water, and can also produce what the locals call "widowers"—giant tree branches that can fall without warning on anyone below. Locals advise against hiking or camping under trees in these conditions.

The ocean can be just as unpredictable and dangerous here if you're not paying attention. This region is prone to "sneaker waves," powerful and potentially deadly waves that surge farther onto shore than expected, knocking down and pulling unsuspecting beachgoers into the frigid Pacific waters. As a precaution, you can check the National Weather Service website for high surf warnings, but sneaker waves can occur without warning even on calm days and under favorable conditions, so it is important to

never let your guard down, never turn your back to the ocean, and keep your eye on the waves even when they are small. Avoid areas with active breaking waves and waves more than 3 feet high. Beaches with a lot of rocks, sea stacks, and beach debris like giant logs can be especially dangerous if you are pulled in by a sneaker wave; you're much safer walking or picnicking farther from the water on dry sand. If visiting with children, be sure they stay near adults and consider having them wear life vests when playing near the ocean. Be aware of the tide schedule when hiking down cliffs to beaches or tidepooling so you aren't caught by surprise as the tide comes in.

Cell phone service can be limited, so it's important to download maps to your devices before you arrive. If traveling during winter or early spring, pack a poncho, a rain jacket, a wet bag, footwear with a good grip, an extra pair of dry socks, and anything else needed to protect your body and personal items from the rain. If traveling in the summer, be sure to pack extra water, comfortable shoes, sun protection, and closed-toe footwear for tidepooling to avoid injury to your feet in this rocky terrain. Medical care options are limited in this region, so make wise choices to stay injury free on your trip.

Educate yourself about the region's history.

After passing through the Redwood Curtain it's easy to get lost in the beauty of these ancient giants and stunning panoramic coastlines, but it's important to educate yourself about the region's history when it comes to human impact on the landscape and the Indigenous and Asian communities that were expelled, displaced, exploited, and harmed here. By visiting local history museums, cultural centers, and visitor centers, and by taking in park interpretive programs and Indigenous-led

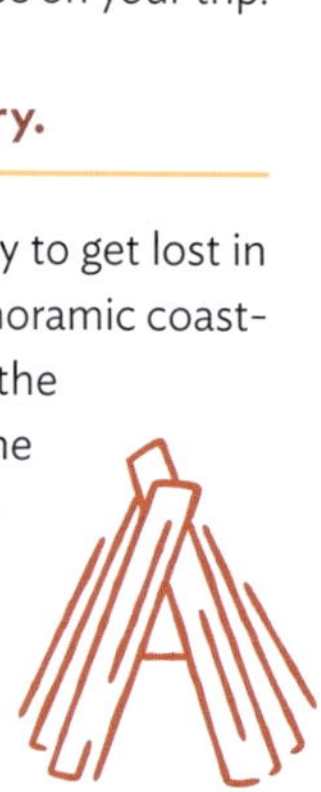

cultural programs in the region, you will gain a broader perspective and understanding. To learn more about the history of the Chinese expulsion in Humboldt County, visit the public art, dedicated site installations, and public programming in Eureka, part of HAPI's Eureka Chinatown Project. Many books on the impacts of logging, Indigenous history, and ecological knowledge from an Indigenous perspective—such as *Ka'm-t'em: A Journey Toward Healing*, excerpted in this book—are available in California state park visitor centers and local bookstores.

Support small businesses and local lodging.

Staying at locally owned hotels, motels, inns, and B&B's, as opposed to chains, is a great way to support local residents and economies. If you are booking through services like Airbnb or VRBO, look to see if your host is a full-time resident and consider that perhaps your stay in their guest bedroom or guesthouse is funding their ability to live here year-round, as many people piece together part-time, low-paying jobs. You can also read their listing or bio to see what they are doing to support the community and environment around them—like maintaining a natural pesticide-free garden, capturing rainwater, or offering composting for guests.

Shopping local is another fun way to support the local economy and get the authentic feel of the region. Buy direct or visit local shops, markets, and restaurants that carry locally produced goods, wares, harvests, and the day's catch. By buying local, you're supporting local families and their livelihoods, and helping to preserve the local culture and community that make this a special place. You're also lessening your environmental impact by reducing the carbon footprint inherent in transportation and shipping, and encouraging sustainable practices within the community.

For any lodging or business, consider reading reviews online to look for comments that might give you pause about how you're spending your dollars and consider if it aligns with your values. For example, have they recently cleared old-growth forest to expand their operations and profit?

Towns to Visit

Arcata is home to Cal Poly Humboldt, known for its environmental science, natural sciences, natural resources management, and oceanography programs—as well as its emphasis on liberal arts and social justice. Be sure to visit the trails in the Arcata Community Forest and the year-round farmer's market at Arcata Plaza on Saturdays. This artsy college town offers lots of options for dining, lodging, and shopping. Rainy day? Get cozy and hang with the locals at Northtown Coffee, then mosey over to Northtown Books. If you're visiting in the summer, stop by the Arcata Bay Oyster Festival and the regular summer concert series and art markets.

Crescent City, rebuilt after the devastating tsunami of 1964, is a gateway to Jedediah Smith Redwoods State Park, as well as a commercial fishing hub. The city offers fish markets and seafood restaurants that span from no frills, low-key establishments along the docks to high-end waterfront dining. Don't miss SeaQuake Brewing's home-brewed beer and kombucha, pizza, and Battery Point snapper—a locally caught Pacific rockfish. The Del Norte County Historical Society Museum is housed in an old sheriff's office and county jail, with two floors of North Coast history, Native American artifacts, antique equipment, and even intact jail cells. Battery Point Lighthouse is a working lighthouse that can be accessed by the public at low tide. Ocean World, a beloved aquarium, features an impressive array of sea life, with up-close views and touch pools.

Eureka, just a hop and a skip from Arcata, is the Humboldt County seat and the oyster capital of Northern California. Considered the market and cultural center of the Redwood Coast, this historic seaport town is filled with Victorian architecture and lots of options for dining, lodging, and shopping. In the summer, the weekly Friday Night Market features performers, musicians, local makers, artisans, farmers, and food vendors. Year-round on the first Saturday of every month, Arts Alive! fills the streets with live music and dancing, and shops and galleries are open late. For a good read, head to Eureka Books, an independent bookstore housed in a historic Victorian-style building, or just down the street to Booklegger for used books and other quirky items. If you're hungry, stop by Gill's by the Bay for seafood with a no-fuss ocean view or go off the beaten path to local favorite Brick & Fire Bistro for pizzas and wild mushroom cobbler.

Ferndale ("Cream City") is best known for its quality dairy products. Thanks to the frequent inundation from overflowing rivers, the nutrient-rich runoff from the mountains, and the year-round fog, Ferndale's cow pastures are green and lush all year. Visit the Ferndale Museum to learn more about the history of its dairy industry, or head to a market for local milk, cheese, and Humboldt Creamery ice cream. Its bright and colorful Victorian architecture puts Ferndale on the National Register of Historic Places. Stroll the main street to browse the shops—including old-timey general store Golden Gait Mercantile and the Ferndale Arts Gallery. Valley Grocery has you covered for delicious deli sandwiches and Mexican food (the torta is *outstanding*). For a truly small-town experience, look over the best of the best dairy cows and livestock at the Humboldt County Fair in August.

Mill Valley is the gateway to Muir Woods National Monument, just a short drive from San Francisco. Explore the Golden Gate National Recreation Area and drive the Panoramic Highway to Mount Tamalpais State Park to access miles of trails and sweeping ocean vistas. Stroll around town to visit upscale shops, restaurants, cafes, and entertainment venues like Sweetwater Music Hall and the restored Throckmorton Theater. In the summer, you can enjoy musical theater al fresco at Mountain Play, an outdoor amphitheater that has been operating on Mount Tam for more than a century. If you need a grocery resupply, consider Mill Valley Market or Good Earth Natural Foods. A must-visit is the Mill Valley Depot Café and Bookstore, the heartbeat of the community. Consider stopping in the nearby seaside town of **Sausalito** to see enclaves of houseboats, hike the trail to Point Bonita Lighthouse, eat fresh seafood at the popular Fish, and pick up a new book dockside at Sausalito Books by the Bay.

Trinidad is a picturesque seaside town nestled right along the rugged coast, with easy access to Sue-meg State Park and Big Lagoon County Park. From the edge of town just steps from its handful of shops and restaurants, you can walk down to Old Home Beach (formerly Indian Beach), where you can go tidepooling and take in views of Trinidad Head and sea stacks. Stroll on the sand at the easily accessible Trinidad State Beach and the more secluded College Cove, and catch the sunset from Moonstone Beach County Park or Luffenholtz Beach County Park. Be sure to stop by the Trinidad Museum to learn about the region's natural and cultural history, as well as the Trinidad Art Gallery, a local artist cooperative gallery and shop. For some really good grub, swing by Trinidad Bay Eatery

& Gallery, stop at Murphy's Market and Deli, or drive out to the more upscale Larrupin' Cafe, a local dinner-only favorite that serves locally sourced dishes. Save room in your suitcase for jars of their mustard dill sauce to bring home—*trust us.*

Where to Camp

Big Lagoon County Park, where you can fall asleep to the sound of waves rolling in off the Pacific Ocean. Twenty-five year-round first-come, first-served dog-friendly campsites with fire pits are just steps away from the ocean, where you can stroll the beach and beachcomb, and walking distance from a freshwater lagoon where you can fish, swim, and paddle a canoe or kayak.

Crescent City / Redwoods KOA Holiday, a 17-acre park offering tent sites, one- and two-room cabins, and full-hookup RV sites among redwood trees and alder groves. A great launching point for adventures in Jedediah Redwoods State Park, Crescent City, or any destinations along the Del Norte coast, this campground offers sites with tables and fire rings as well as bathrooms with flush toilets and warm showers, and amenities like bike rentals, a rec center with Wi-Fi, a playground, an off-leash dog run, and a laundry room.

Florence Keller Regional Park, best suited for smaller RVs and tent campers. The peaceful first-come, first-served dog-friendly campground offers fifty sites nestled among second-growth redwoods with a verdant forest floor and walking trails, and is open all year. Jedediah Smith Redwoods State Park, Del Norte Coast Redwoods State Park, Tolowa Dunes State Park, and Crescent City are all easily accessible by car.

Grizzly Creek Redwoods State Park, for those looking for a lesser-traveled redwood forest or easy river access to fish, swim, or paddle in the Van Duzen River. Nestled within the tiny 400-acre Grizzly Creek Redwoods State Park, the small, secluded seasonal campground stays cool throughout the summer and offers a limited number of reservable tent, RV, and group sites.

Humboldt Redwoods State Park, where you can sleep under the giants in the world's largest old-growth contiguous redwood forest. This 53,000-acre state park boasts more than 250 campsites across its many campgrounds. The seasonal Albee Creek and Hidden Springs Campgrounds and the year-round Burlington Campground are most suitable for family camping. A horse camp, trail camps, and hike-and-bike sites extend the range of options. You can reserve sites six months in advance or as late as forty-eight hours before arriving.

Jedediah Smith Redwoods State Park, a favorite of many who return year after year over decades. You can listen to the soothing Smith River in the park's breathtaking year-round campground located in an old-growth redwood grove, with tent sites, RV sites with no hookups, and four ADA-accessible cabins. The campground, which accepts reservations, has an amphitheater for seasonal campfire programs and easy access to hiking, swimming, and fishing.

Klamath River RV Park, a well-maintained, pet-friendly private campground right along the Klamath River. Boasting spectacular views and ample fishing opportunities, this is an ideal base camp for exploring nearby parks while enjoying amenities that include a laundry room, a playground, and an on-site cafe with coffee and snacks on summer weekends.

Mill Creek Campground, several miles off the highway in a grove of young redwoods and maples in Del Norte Coast Redwoods State Park. This seasonal campground, which accepts reservations, is ideal for tent campers, and sites have fire rings, benches, and bear boxes. Campers have easy access to coastline views and trails, and seasonal programs.

Mystic Forest RV Park, described as a "hidden gem." This small, privately owned campground is just down the road from Trees of Mystery and conveniently located if you plan to sightsee at the mouth of the Klamath River. In addition to RV hookups, it has a few tent sites available in summer and three year-round cabins, as well as a game room, a mini golf course, a laundry room, horseshoe pits, a swing set, and a small camp store.

Prairie Creek Redwoods State Park, with two stunning year-round campgrounds best suited for tent campers and smaller RVs. The campgrounds offer sites with fire pits, picnic tables, and bear boxes, and limited cell reception. Under old-growth trees, Elk Prairie Campground also offers four ADA-accessible cabins and is steps away from grazing Roosevelt elk and black-tailed deer, and easy access to the world's most extensive system of trails through the redwoods. Gold Bluffs Beach Campground is situated right along the bluffs of the Pacific Ocean, close to secluded beaches, the Coastal Trail, and Fern Canyon. While dogs are permitted in the campgrounds and on the beach, they're not permitted on any park trails and cannot be left unattended.

Sue-meg State Park, with tons of campsites available for those wanting to explore both lush forests and coastal trails. The seasonal

Abalone Campground offers tent, RV, and trailer sites in the shade of the forest right next to breathtaking coastal viewpoints and trails. Year-round Agate Beach Campground sits along the coast and offers five ADA-accessible cabins in addition to tent, RV, and trailer sites. The seasonal Penn Creek Campground offers fourteen tent-only sites arranged in a single loop. Pets are permitted in all camping and picnic areas but not on any trails or beaches.

In addition to these public campgrounds, you can also arrange campsites through camping companies, such as Hipcamp, that provide access to private land and campsites while supporting local communities and preserving natural spaces.

Community Resources

Humboldt Asians and Pacific Islanders in Solidarity (HAPI) formed organically in 2021 from the recognition that Asians and Pacific Islanders in Humboldt County were excited to connect and develop community. HAPI leads the Eureka Chinatown Project, aimed at honoring and celebrating the history and culture of the first Chinese people, who made huge contributions and were expelled from Eureka in 1885. Members of HAPI believe that by educating the community—through community gatherings, panel discussions, collaborative projects, speakers and performances, food, and sharing cultural traditions and celebrations—this community can heal and participate in creating a more inclusive and just future.
hapihumboldt.org

Northeast Environmental Center (NEC) is dedicated to conserving and restoring the natural environment of Northern California and southern Oregon through advocacy, education, and community engagement. Its mission is to promote understanding of the relations between people and the biosphere, and its team conducts habitat restoration projects, influences environmental policy, promotes sustainable practices, and offers educational programs.
yournec.org

Northern California Condor Restoration Program (NCCRP) is a collaborative effort between the Yurok Tribe, the National Park Service, and the US Fish and Wildlife Service to restore the endangered condor to Yurok ancestral territory and the Pacific Northwest. The Yurok Condor Restoration Program (YCRP), which is part of the NCCRP, is aimed at reestablishing a population of condors, which have been absent for more than a century due to Euro-American colonization and destruction of their habitat, to ensure condors can play a crucial role in restoring the region's ecological health, balance, and biodiversity.
yuroktribe.org/yurok-condor-restoration-program

Redwood Parks Conservancy (RPC) is a leader in the preservation and enhancement of natural and cultural resources in Northern California parks. Its work led to the 2022 opening of the Grove of Titans and its sustainable boardwalk trails in Jedediah Smith Redwoods State Park, the reintroduction of the California condor and restoration of its habitat in collaboration with the Yurok tribe, and memorable events in the parks including an annual candlelight walk, a 5k run, and a 5th of July beach cleanup. In addition to making a donation, you can support the Conservancy by making a purchase at any of the many stores it operates in park visitor centers and online.
redwoodparksconservancy.org

Redwoods Rising is a large-scale effort and partnership between California State Parks, the National Park Service, and Save the Redwoods League to restore areas damaged by historical logging in Redwood National and State Parks.
nps.gov/redw/redwoodsrisingmain.htm

Save the Redwoods League is a storied nonprofit credited with saving more than 200,000 acres of redwood forest by purchasing land and getting national and state parks and preserves established to protect them in the early 1900s. Though its founders have a complicated past, as acknowledged by the organization today, the league is still a major player working in collaboration with Indigenous tribes, parks, national and state agencies, and other organizations to not only preserve and restore redwood forest by purchasing and protecting land but also to provide equitable access and education about these parks, and to do crucial research on redwoods and climate change.
savetheredwoods.org

Essential Reads

Journey to Mount Tamalpais
by Etel Adnan (Litmus Press, 2021)

Passing the Moon Through 13 Baskets: A Guide to the Natural Year and Native American Celebrations on the Wild Redwood Coast
by Susan Calla with Sandra Jerabek and Loren Bommelyn (Redwood Economic Development Institute, 2005)

The Sound of Fish Dreaming
by Benjamin Green (Bellowing Ark Press, 1995)

The Legacy of Luna: The Story of a Tree, a Woman, and the Struggle to Save the Redwoods
by Julia Butterfly Hill (HarperSanFrancisco, 2000)

Totem Salmon: Life Lessons from Another Species
by Freeman House (Beacon Press, 2000)

Ka'm-t'em: A Journey Toward Healing
by Dr. Kishan Lara-Cooper and Walter J. Lara Sr. (Great Oak Press, 2019)

The Overstory: A Novel
by Richard Powers (Norton, 2019)

The Wild Trees: A Story of Passion and Daring
by Richard Preston (Random House, 2007)

Walking in Beauty: Growing Up with the Yurok Indians
by Harry K. Roberts (Trinidad Art, 2016)

Becoming Story: A Journey Among Seasons, Places, Trees, and Ancestors
by Greg Sarris (Heyday Books, 2022)

The Once and Future Forest: California's Iconic Redwoods
by Save the Redwoods League (Heyday Books, 2021)

Acknowledgments

Working on this book series as parents to two young kids has required a village. Ilyssa, first and foremost, would like to thank Dave for supporting and encouraging her enthusiasm for this new *Campfire Stories* series and her decision to *not* plow right into a new job. With Ilyssa taking the lead on travel to research these books, Dave took on the primary responsibility for cooking every meal, doing every school or activity drop-off and pickup for two kids at two different schools, conducting the bedtime routine *every night*, and generally keeping our kids alive, full of snacks, and happy—often for a week at a time. Without Dave's unwavering belief in Ilyssa's passion and ideas, in addition to his editing and writing contributions, there would be no *Campfire Stories.* We'd also like to thank Ilyssa's mom, Diane Shapiro, who supports us during these times of travel and writing—and our many friends who host the girls for playdates and sleepovers.

Our daughters, Lula and Isla, also deserve thanks for inspiring us to pursue our passions and for their patience and understanding when we have to travel—even when it makes them feel like *a barnacle drifting all alone at sea.*

We are so grateful to Kate Rogers, editor in chief of Mountaineers Books, who curiously continues to entertain our *many* ideas, and—with honesty and great wisdom—helps to refine and shepherd them into the world. We extend this appreciation to the rest of the Mountaineers Books team, whose enthusiasm for our projects is deeply felt—and with a special shout-out to Joleen, who makes us feel like rock stars. To our editing team, Beth Jusino and Lorraine Anderson—we are grateful for your meticulous editorial work, and we admire your ability to take on a massive collection of stories spanning many centuries with enthusiasm and patience.

This series would not be what it is without Melissa McFeeeters, who has been with us from the very beginning and has designed all of our *Campfire Stories* projects—likely the reason you, reader, picked up our book in the first place!

We'd also like to thank the writers, librarians, researchers, and staff and/or volunteers of the many nonprofit organizations and museums we've connected with across the Redwood Coast for your generosity and time. Our understanding of these places would be far less authentic, passionate, and informed without your personal stories, lived experiences and history, and special connections to them. We'd especially like to thank Dan Sealy and Bryan Vinyard for hosting Ilyssa in their beautiful home by the sea and feeding her—and Dan especially, for sharing his knowledge of this region as a former ranger and for connecting us to others whose perspectives and voices often go underrepresented. We have so much gratitude for Mia Monroe, who chose to spend a couple of hours with us and gift us with her wisdom and enthusiasm for Muir Woods on her final day of work after more than fifty years volunteering and working for the National Park Service. We are grateful to Carly Marino and Sarah Godlin at the Cal Poly Humboldt Library Special Collections and Archives for their recommendations and insights into the stories of this region. We'd also like to thank Victor Bjelajac of California State Parks / North Coast Redwoods for his time, perspective, and dedication to elevate and seek justice, partnership, and collaboration with the region's Indigenous tribes. We appreciate Marnin Robbins of California Department of Fish and Wildlife for sharing his joy and depth of knowledge while strolling with us through the Arcata Community Forest. Last, we'd like to shout out to Vicki Ozaki, who joined us on a hike to share her experience of working with the Park Service restoring the forest and streams, and educated us about the often-untold history of the brutal expulsion of the region's Chinese community—as well as her work to celebrate and revive that culture and history in Humboldt County today.

To the bookstore buyers and staff who take time to chat with us while we're on our research trips, who educate us on local writers and important literature as well as carve a little space on your shelves for our book or feature it in your beautiful, creative displays—we see you and we appreciate you. We can't express how delighted we are to receive texts from friends and family traveling across the US who spot our books or card decks in the wild, or when we ourselves encounter them in real life. It never gets old.

Last, to our dear readers, whose insatiable desire for stories from our wild places allows us to continue collecting stories—we are grateful for your curiosity, love for our natural world, and desire to follow in the age-old tradition of storytelling. Without those readers who reached out or attended our events to say, *When are you going to do MY favorite place in the world?* or challenged us to consider places outside of national parks, we wouldn't have embarked on this new series.

Permissions and Sources

Permissions

"At the Center of the Earth." Printed with the permission of the Tolowa Dee-ni' Nation.

Bourbeau, Heather. "Restoration." Printed with the permission of the author.

Chinn, Daryl Ngee. "The Heartwood Life of Questions." Printed with the permission of the author.

Samuel Green, "Island Potluck" from *Disturbing the Light*. Copyright © 2019 by Samuel Green. Reprinted with the permission of The Permissions Company, LLC on behalf of Carnegie Mellon University Press.

Hart, John. "Redwood Forest." Printed with the permission of the author.

"The Legacy of Luna" from *Legacy of Luna* by Julia Hill. Copyright © 2000 by Julia Butterfly Hill. Used by permission of HarperCollins Publishers.

Holland, Annette Boushey. "The Woman Who Saved Founders Grove." Printed with the permission of the author.

Holper, David. "Hiking the Skunk Cabbage Trail," originally published in *Third Wednesday*, May 2012. Printed with the permission of the author.

Holper, David. "Hyperion," originally published in *Synkroniciti, Wild Issue*, 2023. Printed with the permission of the author.

Lara, Callie. "I Am a Visitor of the Forest." Originally published in *KA'M-T'EM: A Journey Toward Healing*, copyright © 2019. Used with the permission of the family and Great Oak Press. All rights reserved.

Lara, Callie. "Songs of 'Those Within.'" Originally published in *KA'M-T'EM: A Journey Toward Healing*, copyright © 2019. Used with the permission of the family and Great Oak Press. All rights reserved.

Martien, Jerry. "What We Save." Printed with permission of the author.

McCovey, Shaunna Oteka. "We Who Hold Up the World." Printed with the permission of the author.

Excerpt(s) from *The Wild Trees: A Story of Passion and Daring* by Richard Preston, copyright © 2007 by Richard Preston. Used by permission of Random House, an imprint and division of Penguin Random House LLC. All rights reserved.

Sarris, Greg. "The Ancient Ones." Originally published in *Becoming Story: A Journey Among Seasons, Places, Trees, and Ancestors*, copyright © 2022. Printed with permission of Heyday Books.

The editors have made every effort to locate all copyright holders for the excerpts in this book. In some cases, however, they were unable to locate the appropriate person or entity, or to confirm the publication date or other relevant details. If anyone has information on any of the poems, stories, or essays included here, please contact the editors at hello@campfirestoriesbook.com

Sources

"Enjoying the Beach: Tips to Stay Safe While Enjoying the North Coast." Redwood National and State Parks, 2006, www.nps.gov/redw/planyourvisit/upload/BeachSafety-Dec06-508.pdf.

"Fishing in Redwood National and State Parks." National Park Service, www.nps.gov/articles/fishing-in-redwood-national-and-state-parks.htm.

French, Susan M. J. "A Glimpse into the Life of Harriet E. Weaver." Fillmore Historical Museum website, 26 August 2020, www.fillmorehistoricalmuseum.org/harriett-petey-weaver.

Gronlund, Melissa. "California Soul: Exploring Etel Adnan's West Coast Vision." Sothebys.com, 17 March 2022, www.sothebys.com/en/articles/california-soul-exploring-etel-adnans-west-coast-vision.

"Grove of Titans: Traditional Native Land." Save the Redwoods League, 10 September 2021, www.savetheredwoods.org/project/grove-of-titans/traditional-native-land.

Hoover, Kevin. "Susie Van Kirk and Lucille Vinyard: Partners in Activism, Friends to the End." *Mad River Union*, 6 January 2016, www.madriverunion.com/articles/susie-van-kirk-and-lucille-vinyard-partners-in-activism-friends-to-the-end.

"Klamath River." American Rivers, www.americanrivers.org/river/klamath-river.

Klingenberg, Susanna. "5 Ways to Chase Awe at Muir Woods National Monument." National Parks Conservation Association, 2 January 2024, www.npca.org/articles/3677-5-ways-to-chase-awe-at-muir-woods-national-monument.

"Mission and History." Save the Redwoods League, www.savetheredwoods.org/about-us/mission-history.

"Our Story." Humboldt Creamery, www.humboldtcreamery.com/our-story.

Reilly, Janet. "Greg Sarris on Tribal Leadership and a Sense of Belonging." *Nob Hill Gazette*, 28 May 2024, www.nobhillgazette.com/people/the_interview/greg-sarris-on-tribal-leadership-and-a-sense-of-belonging/article_f30ba18c-13b0-11ef-9bf0-9b5b88792951.html.

"Seven Steps That May Save Your Life." Cal Poly Humboldt, Redwood Coast Tsunami Work Group, rctwg.humboldt.edu/prepare/seven-steps.

"Smith River." National Wild and Scenic Rivers System, www.rivers.gov/river/smith.

Stenger, Richard. "Make a Big Splash Among the Big Trees." Save the Redwoods League, 9 June 2014, www.savetheredwoods.org/blog/make-a-big-splash-among-the-big-trees.

"Tidepool Animals." National Park Service, www.nps.gov/redw/learn/nature/tidepool-animals.htm.

Viloria, Dana. "10 Rules of the Redwood Forest." Save the Redwoods League, 14 August 2019, www.savetheredwoods.org/blog/10-rules-of-the-redwood-forest.

"Who We Are." Resighini Ranchería, resighinirancheria.com/who-we-are.

"You Live in Earthquake Country." Cal Poly Humboldt, Redwood Coast Tsunami Work Group, rctwg.humboldt.edu/earthquakes/earthquake-country.

"Yurok Tribe and California State Parks Sign Historic Memorandum of Understanding." Yurok Tribe, 28 September 2022, www.yuroktribe.org/post/yurok-tribe-and-california-state-parks-sign-historic-memorandum-of-understanding.

Directory

MARIN COUNTY

Golden Gate National Recreation Area
nps.gov/goga

Muir Beach Overlook
nps.gov/goga/planyourvisit/muirbeach.htm
Seacape Dr, Muir Beach

Stinson Beach
nps.gov/goga/stbe.htm
3514 Shoreline Hwy, Stinson Beach

Mill Valley
enjoymillvalley.com

142 Throckmorton Theatre
throckmortontheatre.org
142 Throckmorton Ave

Dipsea Trail
onetam.org/maps-trails/dipsea-trail
Trailhead at Old Mill Park, Cascade Dr and Molino Ave

Good Earth Natural Foods
shop.genatural.com/stores/good-earth-natural-foods-mill-valley
201 Flamingo Rd

Mill Valley Depot Café and Bookstore
depotcafeandbookstore.com
87 Throckmorton Ave

Mill Valley Film Festival
mvff.com
Various venues, including Sequoia Cinema, 25 Throckmorton Ave

Mill Valley Music Festival
millvalleymusicfest.com
Friends Field, 180 Camino Alto

Mill Valley Public Library
millvalleylibrary.org
375 Throckmorton Ave

Mount Tamalpais State Park
parks.ca.gov/?page_id=471
801 Panoramic Hwy

Mountain Play
mountainplay.org
Cushing Memorial Amphitheater in Mount Tamalpais State Park
East Ridgecrest Blvd

Muir Woods National Monument
nps.gov/muwo/index.htm
1 Muir Woods Rd

Steep Ravine Trail
parks.ca.gov/?page_id=471
Mount Tamalpais State Park
Trailhead at Pantoll Campground parking lot, 6456 Panoramic Hwy

Sweetwater Music Hall
sweetwatermusichall.com
19 Corte Madera Ave

Tennessee Valley
nps.gov/goga/planyourvisit/tennessee_valley.htm
591 Tennessee Valley Rd

Sausalito
visitsausalito.org

Fish
331fish.com
350 Harbor Dr

Point Bonita Lighthouse and Trail
nps.gov/goga/pobo.htm
Marin Headlands,
Field Rd and Conzelman Rd

Sausalito Books by the Bay
sausalitobooksbythebay.com
100 Bay St

Sausalito Houseboats
oursausalito.com/houseboats/houseboats-in-sausalito.html
Park near Issaquah Dock and Liberty Dock

HUMBOLDT COUNTY

Arcata
visitarcata.com

Arcata Bay Oyster Festival
arcatabayoysterfestival.com
Arcata Plaza, 844 H St

Arcata Community Forest
cityofarcata.org/190/City-Forests
14th and Union St

Arcata Plaza
cityofarcata.org/883/Plaza-Events
844 H St

Arcata Plaza Farmers' Market
northcoastgrowersassociation.org/arcataplaza.html
Saturdays at Arcata Plaza,
844 H St

Mad River Fish Hatchery
wildlife.ca.gov/Fishing/Hatcheries/Mad-River
1660 Hatchery Rd

Northtown Books
northtownbooks.com
957 H St

Northtown Coffee
organicnorthtown.com
1603 G St

Eureka
visiteureka.com

Blue Ox Millworks and Historic Village
blueoxmill.com
1 X St

Booklegger
facebook.com/p/Booklegger-100064419350168
402 2nd St

Brick & Fire Bistro
brickandfirebistro.com
1630 F St

Charlie Moon Way and "Fowl" mural by David Young Kim
hapihumboldt.org/eureka-chinatown-project
Alley between E and F St and 4th and 5th St

Clarke Historical Museum
clarkemuseum.org
240 E St

Eureka Books
eurekabookshop.com
426 2nd St

Eureka Friday Night Market
fridaynight.market
Summer Fridays in Old Town

Freshwater County Park
humboldtgov.org/Facilities/Facility/Details/Freshwater-6
3100 Freshwater Rd

Gill's by the Bay
gillsbythebay.com
77 Halibut Ave

Ferndale
visitferndale.com

Ferndale Arts Gallery
ferndalearts.com
535 Main St

Ferndale Museum
ferndalemuseum.com
515 Shaw Ave

Golden Gait Mercantile
goldengaitmercantile.com
421 Main St

Headwaters Forest Reserve
blm.gov/programs/national-conservation-lands/california/headwaters-forest-reserve
Elk River Rd and Headwaters Forest Trail, South Bay

Humboldt County Fair
humboldtcountyfair.org
Humboldt County Fairgrounds, 1250 5th St

Valley Grocery
visitferndale.com/shopping-business-directory/valley-grocery
339 Main St

Van Duzen County Park
humboldtgov.org/Facilities/Facility/Details/Van-Duzen-Pamplin-Grove-16
Hwy 36, Carlotta

Orick
orick.net

Bald Hills Scenic Drive
nps.gov/thingstodo/drivebaldhillsrd.htm
Prairie Creek Redwoods State Park

Big Tree Loop
parks.ca.gov/?page_id=415
Via Karl Knapp and Cathedral Trees Trails
Trailhead at Prairie Creek Redwoods State Park visitor center

Fern Canyon Loop Trail
nps.gov/places/ferncanyon.htm
Trailhead at Prairie Creek Redwoods State Park visitor center

Gold Bluffs Beach
nps.gov/places/gbbdayuse.htm
Davison Road, Prairie Creek Redwoods State Park

Lady Bird Johnson Grove Trail
nps.gov/places/lbjtrailhead.htm
Trailhead on Bald Hills Rd, Redwood National Park

Newton B. Drury Scenic Parkway
nps.gov/thingstodo/drivenbdparkway.htm
Prairie Creek Redwoods State Park, exit 765 or 753 off of Hwy 101

Prairie Creek Redwoods State Park
parks.ca.gov/?page_id=415
Visitor center, 127011 Newton B. Drury Parkway

Redwood National Park
nps.gov/redw/index.htm
Thomas H. Kuchel Visitor Center, 119441 Hwy 101

Skunk Cabbage Trail
nps.gov/places/skunkcabbsth.htm
Trailhead on Robinson Road off Hwy 101, Redwood National Park

Tall Trees Grove
nps.gov/thingstodo/talltreeshike.htm
Tall Trees Access Rd, McKinleyville

Trillium Falls Trail
nps.gov/places/trilliumfallstrail.htm
Trailhead at Elk Meadow Day Use Area off Davison Road, Redwood National Park

Trinidad
exploretrinidadca.com

Agate Beach
parks.ca.gov/?page_id=28289
North end of Sue-meg State Park, 4150 Patrick's Point Dr

Big Lagoon County Park
humboldtgov.org/Facilities/Facility/Details/Big-Lagoon-County-Park-2
510 Big Lagoon Park Rd

Camel Rock at Houda Point Beach
trinidadcoastallandtrust.org/houda-point.html
1808 Trinidad Scenic Dr

Chah-pekw O' Ket'-toh (Stone Lagoon) Visitor Center
parks.ca.gov/?page_id=30898
15336 Hwy 101

College Cove
parks.ca.gov/?page_id=418
North cove of Trinidad State Beach, 585 Stagecoach Rd

Larrupin' Cafe
thelarrupin.com
1658 Patrick's Point Dr

Luffenholtz Beach County Park
trinidadcoastallandtrust.org/luffenholtz-beach-and-tepona-point.html
1639 Trinidad Scenic Dr

Moonstone Beach County Park
humboldtgov.org/1449/Moonstone-Beach-County-Park
100 Moonstone Beach Rd

Murphy's Market and Deli
murphysmarkets.net
1 Main St

Old Home Beach
trinidadcoastallandtrust.org/parker-creek-trail-to-old-home-beach.html
Trailhead at Trinity and Edwards St

Palmer's Point Beach
parks.ca.gov/?page_id=28289
South end of Sue-meg State Park, 4150 Patrick's Point Dr

Rim Trail
parks.ca.gov/sue-meg
Trailheads on Palmer's Point Rd and Park Entrance Rd, Sue-meg State Park

Seascape Restaurant
seascapetrinidad.squarespace.com
1 Bay St

Sue-meg State Park
parks.ca.gov/sue-meg
4150 Patrick's Point Dr

Sumêg Village
parks.ca.gov/?page_id=28291
Park Entrance Rd, Sue-meg State Park

Telonicher Marine Lab at Cal Poly Humboldt
marinelab.humboldt.edu/visit/info
570 Ewing St

Trinidad Art Gallery
trinidadartgallery.com
490 Trinity St

Trinidad Bay Eatery & Gallery
trinidadeatery.com
607 Parker St

Trinidad Head Loop Trail
hikingproject.com/trail/7029864/trinidad-head-trail
Trailhead at 150 Patrick's Point Dr

Trinidad Museum
facebook.com/TrinidadMuseum
400 Janis Ct

Trinidad Pier
visitcalifornia.com/experience/trinidad-pier
1 Bay St

Trinidad State Beach
parks.ca.gov/?page_id=418
Stagecoach Rd and Main St

Wedding Rock
parks.ca.gov/sue-meg
Trailhead on Wedding Rock Rd, Sue-meg State Park

SOUTHERN HUMBOLDT

visithumboldt.com/location/southern-humboldt

Avenue of the Giants
humboldtredwoods.org
State Rte 254, Humboldt Redwoods State Park

Founders Grove
parks.ca.gov/?page_id=31000
Dyerville Loop Road, Humboldt Redwoods State Park

Humboldt Redwoods State Park
humboldtredwoods.org
Visitor center, Avenue of the Giants, Myers Flat

Rockefeller Forest
parks.ca.gov/?page_id=31000
Lower Bull Creek Flats Rd,
Humboldt Redwoods State Park

DEL NORTE COUNTY

Crescent City
visitdelnortecounty.com

Battery Point Lighthouse
delnortehistory.org/battery-point-lighthouse
Lighthouse Wy

Boy Scout Tree Trail
nps.gov/places/boyscouttreetrail.htm
Trailhead on Howland Hill Rd,
Jedediah Smith Redwoods State Park

Crescent Beach Overlook
nps.gov/places/cresbeachoverlook.htm
Enderts Beach Rd

Del Norte Coast Redwoods State Park
parks.ca.gov/?page_id=414
Hwy 101

Del Norte County Historical Society Museum
delnortehistory.org
577 H St

Enderts Beach
nps.gov/places/endertsbeach.htm
nps.gov/thingstodo/tidepoolendert.htm
Enderts Beach Rd

Grove of Titans
nps.gov/places/got.htm
Howland Hill Rd, Jedediah Smith
Redwoods State Park

Jedediah Smith Redwoods State Park
parks.ca.gov/?page_id=31007
Hwy 199

Klamath River Overlook
nps.gov/places/klamathriveroverlook.htm
Take Requa Rd from Hwy 101,
Klamath

Ocean World
oceanworldonline.com
304 Hwy 101 South

Pebble Beach
visitdelnortecounty.com/see/beaches
N Pebble Beach Dr

SeaQuake Brewing
seaquakebrewing.com
400 Front St

Stout Memorial Grove
nps.gov/places/stoutgrove.htm
Hwy 199, Jedediah Smith
Redwoods State Park

South Beach
visitdelnortecounty.com/see/beaches/
245 Anchor Wy

Tolowa Dunes State Park
parks.ca.gov/?page_id=430
Kellogg Rd

Trees of Mystery
treesofmystery.net
15500 Hwy 101, Klamath

Yurok Canoe Tours
visityurokcountry.com/adventure
Yurok Visitor Center,
101 Klamath Blvd, Klamath

About the Contributors

Heather Bourbeau is a writer of award-winning poetry and fiction featured in many publications and special collections, and nominated for Pushcart Prizes. She has worked with various UN agencies, including the UN peacekeeping mission in Liberia and UNICEF Somalia. Her 2022 collection *Some Days The Bird* is a poetry conversation with the Irish-Australian poet Anne Casey. Her latest collection, *Monarch*, examines overlooked histories from the US West.

Daryl Ngee Chinn has lived in Humboldt County since 1975 and has had his poems published in anthologies and self-published chapbooks as well as his 1989 book *Soft Parts of the Back* and on a monument in Eureka, California, commemorating the 1885 Chinese expulsion and the current Asian American community. Chinn was born in Salt Lake City and traces his family back to the Toisan region of Guangdong Province in China.

Benjamin Green is a second-generation native Californian who earned a bachelor's degree at Humboldt State University and lived for many years in Trinidad on the North Coast, where he was a member of the Ferndale Arts Cooperative. He is the author of eleven books, including *The Sound of Fish Dreaming* and the forthcoming *Old Man Looking through a Window at Night* and *His Only Merit*.

John Hart, an award-winning environmental journalist and poet, got his start after college writing stories for the Marin County Pacific Sun in 1970. Since then, he has authored sixteen books and published hundreds of other works about San Francisco Bay, the Mono Lake preservation controversy, and farmland protection—including *Muir Woods National Monument, An Island in Time: 50 Years of Point Reyes National Seashore, The Climbers,* and *San Francisco's Wilderness Next Door.*

Julia Butterfly Hill is an author, artist, spiritual activist, and life coach who brought international attention to the plight of the ancient redwoods by living for 738 days in the canopy of a tree she named Luna. After her tree sit, she founded the nonprofit Circle of Life, which is committed to transforming human interactions with nature, and wrote *The Legacy of Luna* and *Becoming: Pictures, Poems, and Stories,* as well as coauthoring *One Makes the Difference.*

Annette B. Holland lives with her husband and two horses on a scrap of second and third-growth redwood forest in Northern California. She enjoys writing, painting, hiking, puttering in the garden, and hosting meditation retreats in their remodeled barn. Early in her career, she worked as a staff writer for The Nature Conservancy and taught English composition. She later helped establish two land trusts and served for two decades on the Board of Councilors of Save the Redwoods League. Her publications include articles on environmental issues, short memoirs, and poems.

David Holper lives in Eureka, California, where he served as the first poet laureate of the town from 2019 to 2021. With an MFA from U Mass, he teaches English at College of the Redwoods and has published three volumes of poetry, including *Language Lessons: A Linguistic Hejira, The Bridge,* and *64 Questions.*

Callie Lara (1952–2024) was a Hupa and Karuk regalia maker, storyteller, writer, and teacher, and a member of the federally recognized Hoopa Valley Tribe. She dedicated her life to preserving the philosophy and teachings of Native people along the Redwood Coast, carried on by her family through Ka'm-t'em (kamtem-indigenousknowledge.com). In addition, she also worked for the Child and Family Services Department of United Indian Health Services; the Hupa Culture, Language, and Education program of the Hoopa Valley Tribe; and the Department of Health and Human Services.

Jerry Martien lives in Elk River, California, where he moved with his wife just as Maxxam Corporation was liquidating the last groves of old-growth coastal redwoods, and has worked as a night watchman, truck driver, bookstore clerk, carpenter. He has been writing essays about trees since the 1970's, and has published two histories of money, from shell currency to marijuana, and is completing a fourth collection of poetry.

Shaunna Oteka McCovey is an advocate, poet, and author of *The Smokehouse Boys*. She is Yurok and Karuk, and a member of the Yurok Tribe. She is a graduate of Humboldt State University (Cal Poly Humboldt) where she is a Distinguished Alumni; holds a master's degree in social work from Arizona State University; earned both a master's degree in environmental law and policy and a Juris Doctorate from Vermont Law School; and received an Honorary Doctorate from Marlboro College for her contributions to poetry and her Tribal people.

Richard Preston is the author of ten books of fiction and nonfiction revealing hidden worlds of nature, including *The Hot Zone* and *The Demon in the Freezer*. All of his nonfiction books have first appeared as articles in the *New Yorker*. It was a writing course taught by author John McPhee that Preston took while earning a PhD in English at Princeton that inspired him to realize that nonfiction writing can be literature.

Harry K. Roberts (1906–1981) was born in the East Bay Area of California and trained in the traditional Yurok way during summers spent at the mouth of the Klamath River between 1917 and the mid-1930s. Later in life he moved to Muir Beach and became involved as an advisor and teacher at the San Francisco Zen Center's Green Gulch Farm, where he put together his book of stories, poems, photographs, and essays, *Walking in Beauty*.

Greg Sarris, chairman of the Federated Tribes of Graton Ranchería and board chair of the Smithsonian's National Museum of the American Indian, received his PhD from Stanford in modern thought and literature and went on to teach there and at UCLA, Loyola Marymount, and Sonoma State University for three-plus decades. He is the author of multiple scholarly books as well as the novels *Grand Avenue* and *Watermelon Nights*, the story cycles *How a Mountain Was Made* and *The Forgetters*, and a memoir, *Becoming Story*.

Harriett E. Weaver (1908–1993) earned a degree in physical education from UCLA in 1930 before going on to teach school and serve as a park ranger during the summers. This provided material for the books she wrote, including *There Stand the Giants*, *California's Giant Trees*, and *Adventures in the Redwoods* (later updated and expanded as *Redwood Country*). She taught science at the junior high school in the small Southern California town of Fillmore for twenty-one years, rising early to work on her writing before going to her job.

About the Editors

Ilyssa Kyu is the founder of Amble, a sabbatical program for creative professionals to take time away with purpose in support of nature conservancies. She is a design researcher and strategist with a degree in industrial design and previously worked at boutique and global design studios. She is currently using her design consulting experience to support nature nonprofits through All Hands, a creative collective, as well as continually dreaming up ways to integrate her love for storytelling and the outdoors.

Dave Kyu is a socially engaged artist and writer. Born in Seoul, South Korea, and raised in the United States, he explores the creative tensions of identity, community, and public space in his work. He has managed public arts projects for the Asian Arts Initiative, Mural Arts, and the City of Philadelphia. His own creative projects have found him commissioning skywriting planes to write messages 10,000 feet above Philadelphia and doing everything Facebook told him to do for a month.

Together, they've created the *Campfire Stories: Volume I*, *Campfire Stories: Volume II*, *Campfire Stories Card Deck*, and *Campfire Stories Card Deck—For Kids!* They were artists-in-residence at Independence National Historical Park as part of the Imagine Your Parks grant—a collaboration between the NEA, the National Park Service, and the Mural Arts Program that resulted in an event, "I Will Hold You in the Light," which brought together six diverse performers responding to the theme of "The Pursuit of Happiness."

MORE CAMPFIRE STORIES

Campfire Stories bring together the beauty of the natural world and the traditions of storytelling across cultures in order to build deeper connections to our public lands.

Tales & Travel Companions:

The Adirondacks
Cape Cod
Chesapeake Bay
The Redwood Coast
The San Juan Islands
Santa Fe & Taos

• ✦ •

Tales from National Parks and Trails:

Campfire Stories
Campfire Stories, Volume II

• ✦ •

Cards to Ignite Imagination:

Campfire Stories Deck
Campfire Stories Deck for Kids!

recreation • lifestyle • conservation

MOUNTAINEERS BOOKS, including its two imprints, Skipstone and Braided River, is a leading publisher of quality outdoor recreation, sustainability, and conservation titles. As a 501(c)(3) nonprofit, we are committed to supporting the environmental and educational goals of our organization by providing expert information on human-powered adventure, sustainable practices at home and on the trail, and preservation of wilderness.

Our publications are made possible through the generosity of donors, and through sales of 700 titles on outdoor recreation, sustainable lifestyle, and conservation. To donate, purchase books, or learn more, visit us online:

MOUNTAINEERS BOOKS
1001 SW Klickitat Way, Suite 201 • Seattle, WA 98134
800-553-4453 • mbooks@mountaineersbooks.org
www.mountaineersbooks.org

An independent nonprofit publisher since 1960